Teaching Law

A Framework for Instructional Mastery

2nd Edition

Nelson P. Miller

Teaching Law—

A Framework for Instructional Mastery (2nd edition)

By Nelson P. Miller

Publisher:
Crown Management LLC – February 2018
1527 Pineridge Drive
Grand Haven, MI 49417
USA

ISBN: 978-0-9980601-8-7

All Rights Reserved
© 2018 Nelson P. Miller
c/o 111 Commerce Avenue S.W.
Grand Rapids, MI 49503
(616) 560-0632

Table of Contents

Introduction		1
Chapter 1:	**Pedagogy**	8

How Students Learn
Introduction.
Study of Teaching.
Traditional Forms.
Positivism.
Behaviorism.
Progressives.
Cognitivism.
Realism.
Constructivism.
Law School Origins.
The Modern Law School.
Reforms.
Motivation.
Conclusion.

Chapter 2:	**Course Objectives**	26

What Students Should Learn
Introduction.
Advantages.
Drafting.
Components.
Course Examples.
Use.

Conclusion.

| Chapter 3: | Syllabi | 40 |

What to Include and Why
Introduction.
Short Form.
Long Form.
Detail.
Curriculum.
Goals.
Professor.
Text.
Policies.
Resources.
Methods.
Paths.
Assessments.
Classroom Technology.
Conclusion.

| Chapter 4: | Lectures | 51 |

How Students Learn from Them
Introduction.
Cognitive Perspectives.
Attention.
Interpretation.
Elaboration.
Generation.
Retrieval.
Other Tips.
Performance.
Conclusion.

| Chapter 5: | Socratic Method | 65 |

Its Most-Effective Uses
Introduction.
Components.

    Attributes.
    Faults.
    Improvement.
    Discussion.
    Conclusion.

Chapter 6:   **Differentiating Instruction**   78
How to Serve More Students
Introduction.
History.
Sensitivity.
Strategies.
Process.
Peers.
Modification.
Metacognition.
Mapping.
Instruction.
Assessment.
Conclusion.

Chapter 7:   **Integrating Instruction**   90
Joining Knowledge to Skills and Ethics
Introduction.
Curriculum.
Subjects.
Mixing.
Modules.
Courses.
Paths.
Cases.
Uses.
Conclusion.

Chapter 8:   **Classroom Displays**   100
Making Learning Visual
Introduction.

Forms.
Challenges.
Research.
Goal.
Attention.
Organization.
Illustration.
Analysis.
Storage.
Planning.
Conclusion.

Chapter 9: Inclusion   111
Sustaining an Inclusive Environment
Introduction.
Experience.
Reform.
Today.
Responsibility.
Model.
Framework.
Classroom.
Conclusion.

Chapter 10: Assessment   121
Creating Student Feedback Loops
Introduction.
Formative Assessment.
Learning.
Summative Assessment.
Drafting.
Validity.
Reliability.
Fairness.
Forms.
Conclusion.

Chapter 11: Multiple-Choice Questions   132
How to Make Them Meaningful
Introduction.
Advantages.
Disadvantages.
Drafting Guide.
The Stem.
The Lead-In.
The Options.
Conclusion.

Chapter 12: Essay Questions   141
Writing to Match Course Objectives
Introduction.
Use.
Components.
Planning.
Fact Patterns.
Question Calls.
Model Answers.
Scoring.
Time.
Variety.
Conclusion.

Chapter 13: Grading   149
Scoring Rubrics and Grade Ranges
Introduction.
Criteria.
Scoring.
Rubrics.
Grades.
Grade Ranges.
Calculating Ranges.
Normalizing.
Conclusion.

Chapter 14: Vision   159
    Experiences and Outcomes
    Introduction.
    Personality.
    Outcomes.
    Successes.
    Significant Learning.
    Exploration.
    Thinking.
    Truth.
    Prediction.
    Skill.
    Practice.
    Purpose.
    Ethics.
    Conclusion.

Acknowledgments   172

Bibliography   173

Appendices   190

A	Bloom's Taxonomy of Educational Objectives	
B	Syllabus Checklist	
C	Exam-Format Checklist	
D	Grading Checklist	
E	Common Language	
F	Glossary	

Introduction

Teaching law is endlessly fascinating. It attracts and engages Supreme Court justices and appellate and trial-court judges from the state and federal courts, managing and name partners from major law firms, trial lawyers who have won multi-million-dollar verdicts, skilled associates with great law careers ahead of them, prosecutors, public defenders, and United States attorneys, and corporate counsel for major multi-national corporations. Teaching law also attracts the harried but highly skilled solo practitioner who somehow finds time to share the practitioner's hard-won skills with students who are new to the craft. In law teaching, the most committed jurists and lawyers the nation has to offer guide, coach, mentor, support, encourage, and challenge many of the nation's best, brightest, and most capable learners of all ages, to acquire knowledge, skills, and attributes on which the nation's survival, shape, and prosperity depend.

So why read a single, concise book on practical aspects of teaching and learning law? First, the satisfaction of teaching law depends in large part on basic competence at it. Teaching law cannot be satisfying when we do it poorly. Teaching law implicates an especially wide range of skills, producing an especially wide range of instruction from marvelously effective to woefully ineffective. Law students evaluate law professors both formally and informally. Law professors and the deans responsible for supporting them read student evaluations. Some evaluators are not kind. As either new adjunct law professors or newly hired full-time faculty members, highly skilled lawyers pour themselves into teaching law expecting the success they have already earned in practice, only to come well short of student appreciation and satisfaction. Law professors who have had teaching success can also suddenly find it strangely absent or elusive. Teaching law is all at once intuitive and trained, natural and unnatural, simple and mystifyingly complex. Rare are those who get it right the first time and keep it right over time, without a more systematic understanding of the nature of teaching and learning.

Student evaluations of law professors show remarkable variation, suggesting remarkable variation in the quality of law professor performance. That variation may be due in part to the fact that most law professors have little or no formal education in teaching. Some researchers studying student evaluations of professors conclude that those evaluations are relatively reliable indicators of teaching effectiveness. Training in the basics of instructional competence can reduce or eliminate some of the more deleterious performance variations. The amount and usefulness of student learning influences student evaluations of professors. It is harder to do something poorly when you understand the difference between good and poor performance. It is easier to do something well when you know what makes that difference. Undoubtedly, some law professors teach successfully without any education in teaching and learning. Study proves it just as true that most professors rate their own performance higher than others rate it and rate the performance of other professors lower than their own. A little humility in assessing one's own teaching prowess can be a very healthy attribute, not only for oneself but also for one's students.

Law school once insulated law professors from consumer and constituent demands of higher education generally. No longer. Burgeoning accountability in higher education, spurred on by dramatic rises in student debt levels, breached law school's citadel. Law professors no longer get a free pass either from accrediting agencies or legal education's direct constituents—the law firms and their clients, courts, agencies, corporate-counsel offices, and other employers of new lawyers, or even the law students who once helped keep their law professors on their pedestals. Competition from within and outside of graduate education, new job demands on lawyers, changes in the economy and financing of graduate education, and changes in the students whom law professors teach, all demand greater skill and accountability from law professors. Even law school's signature pedagogy, the Socratic Method, is under critical attack. Law professors need to know more now than ever about teaching and learning.

Another reason to look for a concise book on competent law teaching is that the scholarly, empirical, and practical literature on teaching and learning is so large, rich, and nuanced. Literature on law teaching is not as extensive or developed but is still valuable, astute, and rapidly growing. The bibliography cites a fraction of it, including not only the Carnegie Foundation report *Educating Lawyers* but also, for another excellent example, the report *Best Practices for Legal Education* from the Clinical Legal Education Association. Instruction on teaching and learning is so vast as to be hard to grasp and appreciate. Dabbling in the literature on course design, course objectives, assessment, or diversified instruction, for instance, may leave you informed in those areas but confused or naïve about other areas like lecture, visual displays, integration of instruction, and grading. The problem is to digest those voluminous writings into something clear, orderly, and above all practical for the instruction of law. Identifying, acquiring, comprehending, and employing the right readings on the right topics to improve one's law teaching takes substantial time—when time is not that of which the professionals who teach law have an abundance. The judge, trial lawyer, managing partner, or young associate, or even the experienced law professor, may simply have too many other commitments to read, for instance, the huge *Handbook of Educational Psychology* for the small treasures it offers on instruction.

Thus, accept this book's glimpse of the whole of that teaching literature, for an orderly and practical guide to improved law teaching. You should gain from it broad but useful insight on the fundamentals of teaching, as educators currently recognize them in the broader educational literature, but applied to law. Given the time, each of us who teach law should on our own explore that broader literature of education. This book provides a framework for that broader exploration, within the peculiar forms, requirements, and adaptations of legal education. It offers a reality check against basic instructional competencies. Readers should grasp instructional competence as applied to law teaching and learning. You should be able to recognize and apply teaching and learning concepts to your law school instruction, to gain your own confidence and the respect of students, colleagues, staff, and administrators. Readers who follow the concepts organized and presented here should be effective legal educators, able to consistently create and sustain meaningful learning environments to positively influence students in their legal education.

The book includes two features to promote that end. First, it spreads *Reflection* boxes throughout the text. Pause and reflect as you read the text. Like any good learner, interact with the text, mulling how its concepts and recommendations are consistent or inconsistent with your experience and practice. The *Reflection* boxes encourage you in that constructive process. Second, each chapter ends with an *Exercise*. You should have something tangible to show for having engaged in this text, some evidence and outcome linked directly to your teaching. If you do the exercises, then you will have that evidence. Indeed, if you do all exercises, then you will have demonstrated comprehensively the integrity of your law teaching, from course objectives through design to assessment and grading. You may then choose to use that substantial evidence of your teaching reflection and reform, for hiring, retention, promotion, and tenure purposes. Your law school may also offer it as institutional evidence of teaching study, innovation, and engagement.

The book's 14 chapters generally follow the law school term. The law school term at my law school is 14 weeks plus an additional week for examination. A law professor could finish the book by reading one chapter each week of the term. The book arranges chapters to address teaching issues that law professors might especially be thinking about in those weeks of the term. For example, the first chapter addresses broader trends and issues in teaching, to give the reader footing in the field. The second chapter deals with course objectives and the next with syllabi, subjects that students and professors think about early in the term. The next chapters address lectures and Socratic Method, two common forms of instruction. The next chapters address differentiating and integrating instruction, as two sides of the same important coin through which professors learn to disassemble a subject into its constituent parts, variegate instruction to serve more learners, and then reassemble the subject into its whole for the greatest embrace by students. Later chapters treat visual displays and inclusion. Toward the end of the book are chapters on assessment (testing) in its two most-common law school forms, multiple-choice and essay questions. The book concludes with a chapter on teaching vision.

The book's bibliography includes a couple hundred publications on which I drew for the concepts and assertions contained in this book. Some passages of this book draw on my own books, book chapters, and articles, some of them co-authored with other law professors. For readability, this book contains no footnotes. And its words are mine alone, although the concepts it promotes and assertions it makes about teaching are not original and are instead largely originated or promoted by others and shared by many. Some passages of this book draw heavily enough on specific sources written by other authors that those passages cite those sources in the text. When you have the time, please consider reading sources cited in the text and bibliography, with others you discover on your own. One concise law-teaching workbook that I especially recommend, for its brevity, clarity, and engaging style, is Professor Vernellia Randall's *Planning for Effective Legal Education*. Another book that I especially recommend, for its contrary length, depth, and variety, is *Techniques for Teaching Law 2* by Gerald Hess, Steven Friedland, Michael Hunter Schwartz, and Sophie Sparrow.

This book also contains several appendices. Three of the appendices are checklists for the recommendations on syllabi, exam format, and grading. The last two appendices list and then define terms commonly understood and used by educators. Lawyers share law language. They do not necessarily share a language of instruction. The fact that lawyers do not necessarily know the language of learning is unfortunate because lawyers are inveterate learners, possessing remarkable powers to acquire, organize, and use new information. Developing and using a learning vocabulary can make learning easier, more efficient, more productive, better, and more fun and engaging. Look at the appendices. Consider the value of literacy in learning.

Here are a few things that this book is not. This book is not about legal method, like Professor Peter Strauss's classic *Legal Methods: Understanding and Using Cases and Statutes*. A reasonably substantial literature on how lawyers perform legal analysis and how law professors should teach students to do so already exists. The book's purpose is not to contribute to the legal-methods literature. Other good books and articles show how students should set learning goals, form, execute, and assess study plans, read and brief cases, memorize, analyze, prepare for a law school exam, survive law school, and integrate their learning into a healthy professional whole. The bibliography cites some of those books, including a few of my own, although I regard the best of those books as Dean Michael Hunter Schwartz's *Expert Learning for Law Students*, for its elaborate prescriptions. This book's audience is not law students, although no harm would accrue to any law student reading it. Some law students bring to law school substantial education and experience in teaching and learning, those students making insightful critics of the teaching methods of law professors. This book is not, like Ronald Eades' book *How to Be a Law Professor*, a book on how to get and keep a teaching job. See, likewise, the American Bar Association book *Becoming a Law Professor: A Candidate's Guide*, declining to suggest how to teach. Professor Eades, while giving good advice on how to get and keep a teaching job, directs his readers to speak with faculty colleagues, attend conferences, and read books on the psychology of learning for teaching tips. This book's purpose is also not primarily for inspiration, like Parker Palmer's widely and appropriately admired classics *To Know as We Are Known* and *The Courage to Teach*. Any inspiration you draw from this book is more likely to be of the prosaic and practical type rather than that of the mystic.

This book is instead for the law professor who has much subject-matter talent but varying and perhaps unschooled or at least uncertain teaching skills and with little time to improve them. This book thus supplies, at least as a primer in part, what Professor Eades recommends in speaking with colleagues, attending teaching conferences, and reading psychology literature. Parker Palmer noted not only that teaching takes courage but also that too many of us too often feel like impostors. If you feel that way occasionally, as most of us who teach do, then this book should make you feel a little less so. When I started teaching law, a colleague, also new, handed me a book on how to be an undergraduate professor. At the time, it was the best resource available for what we needed. My hope is that this book will serve the same general purpose but be more specific and useful for the law school professor or professor teaching law courses in an undergraduate program. My hope is also that it will stimulate you to further investigate these endlessly fascinating subjects of law and learning.

To go beyond competence in law teaching toward mastery, a second volume of this book share a behavioral approach to teaching law about which I learned from a three-year project that Dr. Douglas Johnson and I conceived and directed at my law school campus. Dr. Johnson directs Western Michigan University's Instructional-Design Research lab, as a professor in the university's Psychology Department. Students in his graduate program in organizational behavior observe my law school classes and classes taught by several of my colleagues, to assess and guide our instruction using behavioral-management methods and principles. They also share behavioral-science presentations and texts on which we draw for instructional inspiration and reform. We have changed our law teaching greatly over the project's three years, with strong positive results in student retention and graduate bar passage. Volume II of this book shares those insights for law professors interested in adopting specific methods improving fluent recall and use of law concepts.

Chapter 1

Pedagogy

How Students Learn

Introduction. To teach effectively, one should have a clear idea of how learning occurs. An effective teacher must not only have deep knowledge of the subject matter but also the skill of teaching. Professors whom colleagues regard as average or below-average scholars in their field may yet be excellent teachers when they understand how learning occurs. By contrast, acknowledged discipline masters can be incapable of conveying even a fraction of their brilliance to students if they know little about learning. Indeed, suggesting that masters convey brilliance to students is itself problematic in describing learning, when one better understands the historical trends and schools of thought on teaching and learning. In an information age, professors no longer hold the monopoly on knowledge that they might once have held. In rapidly changing, diversifying, and globalizing businesses, economies, and cultures, professors can less claim to determine the priority knowledge. Professors are no longer gatekeepers granting access to knowledge. They are instead more like guides whose reflective instructional designs nurse students through formative experiences. The most effective professors may even be innovative program developers and entrepreneurial promoters of their newly accessible and responsive designs. These accelerating paradigm shifts suggest that those who teach law should have some sense of where higher-education instruction has been, where it is, and where it may be going. Law teachers should know something, even a very little, of constantly evolving educational theories. Discovering a little of that theory can be the quickest way to convince one of one's own need for teaching reform.

Study of Teaching. *Pedagogy*, meaning the study of teaching the young, is a well-established field. Teachers in primary and secondary schools, and professors in undergraduate programs, attend to their pedagogical practices. Law professors, by contrast, have different opportunities and face different challenges with their older, more experienced, and more self-directed students. *Andragogy* focuses specifically on studying adult learning. Pedagogical practice typically involves the teacher planning and implementing the instruction. Andragogy, as a slightly different study, encourages law professors to engage students in choosing their educational goals, choosing the instructional designs that will achieve those goals, and implementing and assessing their own learning. Of course, the two fields of pedagogy and andragogy overlap. As adolescents use technology to learn more about the world at ever younger ages, andragogy increasingly influences pedagogy to involve younger students more and earlier in shaping their own learning.

Pedagogy is not an isolated or arcane field. You probably know something of its schools of thought from general education and culture, as from some of its more-famous figures. Classical Greek philosopher Socrates (c. 469-399 BC), for instance, today represents a broad school of inquisitive thought, reflected in his well-known statement that "the unexamined life is not worth living." Law professors invoke a quasi-Socratic method for something like that purpose of examining the grounds for deciding cases. Catholic Church father St. Augustine (354-430 AD) today represents another school of educational thought centered on the condition of the learner, who must search for an interior light under instruction sensitized to the learner's education level and learning preferences. Arab philosopher-physician Ibn Tufayl (c. 1005-1185 AD) represents another strand within education, involving a systematic process of reasoned inquiry devoid of materialism and imagery but informed, in tension, by an extra-rational mysticism. British writer-philosopher Mary Wollstonecraft (1759-1797), by championing the education of women, foreshadowed feminist critiques that influence pedagogy today. Other historical figures influencing education include:

- German philosopher Georg Wilhelm Friedrich Hegel (1770-1831) who cast learning as dialectical;
- English political theorist Herbert Spencer (1820-1903) who, influenced by Charles Darwin, cast education as survival of the fittest;
- German philosopher Friedrich Wilhelm Nietzsche (1844-1900) who sought to educate or inform an elite freed of moral influence to pursue power;
- French psychologist Alfred Binet (1857-1911) who pioneered standard measures of intelligence;
- Italian humanitarian Maria Montessori (1870-1952) who designed stimulating environments that produced educational miracles for children previously judged *defective*; and
- American psychologist and education-reformer John Dewey (1859-1952) who connected education to community life in progressive movement.

Do not underestimate the past's power to influence and shape your own teaching practices. Now consider some of the major schools extant today.

Traditional Forms. Classically, professors conceive teaching as stimulating the student's rational examination of transcendent truths, for the student's moral development. In this model, education emphasizes the generational transfer of knowledge *and values* from professor to student. From Confucius and Plato, through Locke and Kant, all the way to John Stuart Mill, educators saw instruction as shaping students into citizens who could participate productively in the community for the general good. Classicists teach to impart knowledge, from teacher to student. Traditional, classical forms of instruction like the textbook and lecture, question-and-answer sessions, student note taking, and mentor programs remain centerpieces in law school. Professors choose, organize, and impart value-based knowledge, while students absorb or otherwise acquire it, mostly passively. Classical knowledge transfer may remain the dominant paradigm for reflexive educators who know little of the rich history and theory of education, and its later reforms.

Reflection
- Do you recognize assigned readings, lectures, note-taking, question and answer, podcasts of audio recording, and fill-in-the-blank tests as primarily knowledge-transfer forms of education?
- Can you think of learning as anything other than knowledge transfer? Your ability to do so may alone make you a better law professor than you would otherwise be without that ability.

Positivism. Several other paradigms for education have long competed with knowledge transfer, even though the reflexive educator might not recognize or be able to articulate them. Positivism and scientific materialism influenced education beginning with Darwin, Spencer, and Huxley. Materialism plainly brought traditional philosophical and spiritual understandings under increasing scrutiny and challenge. Materialism also challenged classical assumptions about teaching and learning. Under materialist influences, education focused less on the learner's developing attributes that promote community welfare and more on what was going on inside and around the learner. Materialism cast the student as an individual organism for study, independent of education's social-welfare ends. By disconnecting education from its traditional aim of forming a responsible citizen, materialism leaves the goals to individual self-fulfillment or self-realization, a paradigm on full display in Butler, Nietzsche, Montessori, and Russell. Materialism planted the seeds of successive movements through behaviorism, cognitive psychology, and constructivism.

What do these theoretical concerns have to do with your teaching? Do not think of them as entirely abstract. They have their manifestations. Tension between traditional and materialist approaches plays itself out in law school classrooms every day at the practical level. Notice these difference between positivist and traditionalist approaches, and, as you do, think how apparent they must be to students studying under them:

Positivist Professor	Traditionalist Professor
Seldom cites authority.	Frequently cites authority.
Frequently discusses effects.	Seldom discusses effects.
Frequently questions assumptions.	Seldom questions assumptions.
Seldom references professionalism.	Refers often to professionalism.
Seldom mentions responsibility.	Frequently mentions responsibility.
Values intellectual inquiry.	Values community relationship.

> *Reflection*
> - Can you see other differences between positivist and traditionalist teaching?
> - Could you now recognize when you are engaging in one form and when another?
> - Examine some of your specific lecture statements and other instructional activities, classifying each as either traditional or positivist. How can you better draw on the powers of each approach?

Behaviorism. Behavioral theories of learning soon heavily influenced traditional and materialist theories. Behaviorism encourages the teacher to think of learning as a process through which the student changes behaviors not temporarily but in ways that persist and not by instinctual responses but by systematized reflection on experience. Never mind the classical virtues or other attributes of the learner or, for that matter, the learner's materialist survival and adaptation. Behaviorism focuses on the discrete performances necessary to achieve specified learning objectives. For the behaviorist, to learn is to behave differently when instruction concludes. Behaviorism concerns itself less with broad ends or means of instruction, if instruction changes the learner in the direction of the specific objective.

Behaviorism helps instructors focus on individual student performances, requiring law professors to somehow bridge from what students can currently do to what students must do in the future. The approach forces professors to articulate specific learning objectives. To the behaviorist, without objectives, instruction has no point, not (for instance) the traditionalist's interest in student moral development. Under behaviorist principles, professors help students achieve learning objectives through shaping environmental stimuli. Robert Mager was a behaviorist whose engaging books on educational objectives heavily influenced generations of educators. Teachers must clearly define the observable behavior expected of students at the instruction's conclusion and must assess progress and adjust instruction accordingly. We are all behaviorists to some extent. A behaviorist would likely modify traditional instruction by, among other things:

- discerning what students can already do before instruction;
- identifying what students should be able to do after instruction;
- assessing the effectiveness of different forms of instruction;
- establishing criteria for successful student performance;
- more frequently assessing (testing) student learning; and
- providing more feedback to students on assessments.

> *Reflection*
> Do you recognize behavioral aspects of your teaching? Do you see how behaviorism as a teaching paradigm can improve instruction?

Progressives. With notable success, Thomas Dewey and sociologist Emile Durkheim bridged materialism's relentless (some would say aimless and potentially destructive) curiosity and softened behaviorism's sterility, to regain some of the traditional concern for education's democratic and communal ends. Dewey's work supported a Progressive Movement of the 1920s and 1930s, re-connecting education to the needs and interests of the community and nation for responsible and learned citizens. Limited access to higher education limited the Movement's impact until federally backed loan programs increased access. The Movement then had its echo in innovative colleges and universities of the 1960s and 1970s. The collaborative-learning, experiential-learning, service-learning, learning-community, study-abroad, and intercultural-learning opportunities so widely encouraged and embraced on college campuses today reflect Dewey's Progressive Movement, as does the integrative, apprenticeship approach of the Carnegie Foundation's report *Educating Lawyers*. Progressivism may also have helped move educators away from the elitism inherent in materialist and behaviorist approaches toward the more student-centered approach reflected by the emerging cognitivist school.

Cognitivism. Cognitive theories of instruction then gradually influenced and in some measure replaced behavioral theories. Cognitivists focus less on behaviors and more on how mental processes influence behaviors. To the cognitivist, the interesting aspect of instruction is how it creates, modifies, or otherwise affects lasting structures within the student's mind. Benjamin Bloom began by identifying six levels of learning (Bloom's Taxonomy of Educational Objectives), starting with knowledge and moving on to comprehension, analysis, application, synthesis, and finally evaluation. Robert Gagne held that instruction follows orderly steps gaining attention (alertness), informing learners of the objective (expectancy), stimulating recall of prior learning (retrieval to working memory), presenting the primary stimulus (selective perception), providing guidance to learning (encoding to long term memory), eliciting performance (responding), providing feedback and assessing performance (reinforcement), and enhancing retention and transfer (cueing retrieval). In the cognitive mode, effective learning requires motivation, organization, planning, communication, meaning, and consistency.

Reflection
- Consider for a moment the last class session that you taught. Either intuitively or by design, did you begin with some attention-getting activity that would trigger in students' minds an existing knowledge schema, perhaps an experience that they had or something that they had always known or recently learned?
- Did you include as part of your start of class some incentive to the learning that was about to take place?
- Did you then share with students how they could organize the learning?
- Did you support their planning (choice of resources, use of time, etc.) in any way?
- What did you do and have students do that increased communication around the learning objectives?
- Did you use examples or exercises that helped students construct comprehensive meaning from the discrete aspects of their studies?

> - And were you consistent in instructional design to promote student recognition and reliance?

Cognitivism promotes these kinds of opportunities to improve one's teaching. The contributions of educational psychologists following cognitive theories of instruction have been substantial. For example, Carl Bereiter discerned that professors unintentionally design instruction to serve students' interests in minimizing study time and cognitive effort. Teachers do the higher-order tasks of setting goals, choosing objectives, prioritizing objectives, designing instruction, and estimating and assessing time spent on task, while students work only on the lower-order tasks of receiving known facts from identified sources and producing known work product within defined time. According to Bereiter, instruction does exactly what employers do *not* need or value. Bereiter showed that professors can help students make large gains by assigning students higher-order tasks of the type that society and employers value. Does your teaching allow room for students to set goals, choose and prioritize objectives, and design or at least choose instruction?

Realism. More recently, cognitive psychologists have shared the educational stage with realists and constructivists. Adherents to the realist school examine the power structures and class relationships within education. To the realist, instructional activities, classroom designs and management, faculty makeup and behavior, and institutional policies all perpetuate the advantages and disadvantages of classes defined by age, sex, disability, race, ethnicity, culture, socioeconomic status, and other categories. Examining these structures can improve access to and opportunity for learning. The way in which professors manage law school courses and classrooms can have a substantial impact on individual students of different affinities or classes. Realist perspectives can improve teaching in law school classrooms.

> *Reflection*
> - What is the power structure of your classroom?
> - To what extent do you share power with students?
> - Which students do you and your designs empower, and which disempower, in your classroom?

> - How do student seating arrangements and speaking opportunities in your class reflect the power structure of your classroom?
> - What indications might suggest that your course and classroom power structure negatively affects student learning?
> - Who is apathetic and who engaged because of how you design instructional activities and manage the classroom?

Constructivism. Adherents to the constructivist school examine how students assemble meaning from the myriad of influences existing inside and outside of the classroom and curriculum. Learning does not simply occur by the transfer of knowledge within the confines of the casebook and classroom. Students assemble their own meaning from a complex of relationships. The professor may not be primary among those knowledge sources. The classroom and assigned materials may also be subsidiary stimuli among many other sources for learning. Constructivist law professors might find many ways in which to help students articulate subtler and more sound, flexible, and genuine concepts within their fields and subjects than traditional forms of classroom instruction. They include:

- assigning relevant fieldwork;

- encouraging students to talk with one another in small breakout groups about personal or family experiences relating to the studied law subject;

- asking students to bring in newspaper and magazine clippings or internet stories about the studied law subject for classroom discussion;

- introducing students to mentors in the field;

- having students keep journals on their methods, challenges, and successes in learning the studied law subject and then having them periodically read aloud in class from their journals; and

- asking two different students each week to start each class speaking about their inspiration and ambition for law practice.

Overall, these evolving, shifting, and overlapping trends have had their cumulative effect on higher-education instruction. They have led to a clear shift in higher-education paradigms. The old paradigm saw professors transferring knowledge to students, while the new paradigm is to help students construct knowledge. The old had professors winnowing students, while the new has professors developing students. The old professor/student relationship was impersonal, while the new is personal. Power has shifted from professor to student. Knowledge has moved from logical and scientific to personal. The old classroom was competitive, while the new is collaborative. The old students were passive, while the new are active. The old climate was conformist, but the new is diverse. Most importantly for our purposes, the old paradigm held that any discipline expert could teach, while the new holds that teaching is sufficiently complex to require substantial training.

> *Reflection*
> Has the above brief description of educational schools and trends convinced you of the value of exploring teaching more deeply?

Law School Origins. While knowing a bit about these general trends in and influences on higher education is helpful, law school pedagogy has its own interesting history and influences, starting with the great treatises on which law students once depended. Aquinas' *Treatise on Law* represents a scholastic law tradition that still has its influence today. Scholastics used Greek philosophical inquiry, in dialectic form, to elucidate and support Christian and other moral principles. They treated law and other subjects as academic disciplines rather than as the basis for apprenticeship within the related trade or profession. We can credit the scholastics for law school and the law scholarship that law schools produce and on which they rest.

> *Reflection*
> - Do you see yourself as a scholar of the law field you teach?
> - What difference do expository writing and speaking make to your law teaching?

The scholastic influence on law teaching spanned the Renaissance into early American law. The early Renaissance embraced great expository law texts like Hugo Grotius' *On the Law of War and Peace* and Samuel Pufendorf's *On the Duty of Man and Citizen According to Natural Law,* treatises that continue to reflect something distinctly modern, even if in the natural and revealed law tradition more so than strictly scholastic works. Indeed, history identifies Pufendorf as the first modern law professor. The progenitor's title, though, belongs to law chronicler William Blackstone whose classic *Commentaries on the Laws of England* became the standard for law studies in England and colonial America. Abraham Lincoln learned law reading Blackstone and Chitty in his failing general store, never having attended law school. Blackstone's *Commentaries* spawned several American imitators, most notably James Kent in the early 1800s and, in the later 1800s, Thomas Cooley, who wrote several voluminous law treatises that were unrivaled classics of their day. Law students also knew Blackstone and Cooley for their clear expository lectures, lore that helps make lecturing a staple of legal education today.

As important as treatises were to early legal education, apprenticeship, not formal instruction, was the central model for legal education from the founding of this country to the mid- to late-1800s. Do not think apprenticeship to be quaint. Experts in professional education today advocate both cognitive and literal apprenticeships as critical to the development of complete and competent professional identity. Law professors can have students participate in frequent role plays rather than simply observe the professor lecturing. Students can write simulated practice products (fee agreements, correspondence, pleadings, etc.) rather than simply lecture notes. They can accompany professors and other lawyers on pro bono work rather than simply meeting the professor to review an outline. They can write the articles and bylaws for a new student organization rather than simply joining classmates for social events. Enterprising professors find many ways for students to apply the knowledge that they acquire from classroom studies, in activities that simulate law practice.

The Modern Law School. The late 1800s brought Harvard Law School Dean Christopher Columbus Langdell's casebook and Socratic-method reforms. Economics spurred those reforms. Seating 100 or more law students before a grand judge or famous lawyer in a single hall was a highly efficient way for the emerging law schools to recruit and train law students. Representative of the Social Darwinism of the day, Langdell saw law as a science, the appellate opinion as the critical data for students to sift, and the students' law school opportunity as a survival of the fittest. Treatises were on the way out. So were clear supporting lectures. The law was not what a lecturer or treatise said but what appellate opinions reflected. Hence, law schools had little need for skilled lecturers or well-crafted treatises. What law schools needed was a supply of appellate opinions and classroom examiners to model analytic thought. Langdell's reforms gradually came to dominate legal education, surviving nearly unchallenged into the 1960s and 1970s. Apprenticeships were gone. Oral examination of apprentices went out with them. Integrated bars required law degrees and written bar examination. Bar examiners wanted to see rigorous analysis, not professional skill around practice models.

One need not look far to see evidence of these influences. Anyone holding a law degree recognizes the Socratic Method. We have all read casebook after casebook, interspersed with sketchy inquiries and notes. At its best, the Harvard reform showed significant method in its madness. Lawyers are analytical. They can possess remarkable intellectual power to recognize patterns and organize data into comprehensive wholes. Yet at its worst, the case-examination method produces many casualties among students who fail for lack of learning support and a profession that may have lost more of its heart, soul, and identity than the American public would want.

> *Reflection*
> Can you recall something positive and then something negative of your own experience of the Langdell's law school?

Reform. Changes in America's social landscape in the 1960s and then Watergate in the early 1970s had distinct impacts on legal education. Critical and feminist legal scholarship challenged some of the legal academy's basic assumptions. Legal education became more interdisciplinary and open to the influences of economics, sociology, cultural studies, and other fields. Law schools also increased ethics and professionalism instruction, clinical instruction, and instruction in legal writing. The American Bar Association supported or, through accreditation standards promulgated and enforced by its Council of the Section of Legal Education and Admissions to the Bar, required these reforms. Many states bars required applicants to pass the Multistate Professional Responsibility Examination. Many state bars adopted performance tests in addition to the nearly ubiquitous Multistate Bar Examination.

> *Reflection*
> - Recall your own legal education. What was your ethics instruction? Was it for credit? Did tenured faculty teach it?
> - Was legal writing taught for credit by tenured faculty? Was your clinical experience for credit and supervised by tenured faculty?

The 2007 Carnegie Foundation report *Educating Lawyers* evaluated the benefits and limitations of these trends. Non-lawyer educators were the report's primary authors. Its best-known author, Lee Shulman, had helped bring about groundbreaking reforms in medical education. The central theme of *Educating Lawyers* was that legal education has three dimensions, knowledge, skills, and ethics, that law schools must better integrate. Law schools instill the methods of formal legal analysis in the first year so effectively that students lose their natural social skills and ethical ambition, while missing important opportunities to place their doctrinal learning in its practice setting. The Carnegie Foundation report made the following four recommendations:

1) *Integrate First-Year Instruction:* The report first recommended moving more of the integrative clinical experiences into the first year of instruction. It urged law teachers to help students see law practice as bringing client matters into *illuminating relationship* with law's central understandings, reconnecting law practice with moral foundations that Langdell, Holmes, and the positivists had sundered. That work must be accomplished in law school's first year or be lost to the power of law school's overly analytic signature pedagogy.

> *Reflection*
> - Are you helping students connect the doctrinal knowledge of your law field to practice skills, while also helping students develop a positive professional identity?
> - Do your students get to practice relevant skills, producing written work and having the opportunity to interact and advocate over the subject? In what ways do they do so? In what ways could they do so more?

> - Do your students get to exhibit their ethical ambition, showing interest, passion, commitment, and care about both the law subject and the future clients whom they will serve? In what ways do they do so? In what ways could they do so more?

2) *Make Learning Visible:* The Carnegie Foundation report's authors recommended another way to offer students the necessary cognitive apprenticeship while enhancing an apprenticeship of professional identity, which is to make learning more visible. Lawyers are, above all, contextual learners. Because they are experts in the law but novices in their clients' matters, they are constantly learning about their clients' lives, businesses, and experience, while bringing to that context their legal framework. Law professors should coach students to become professional learners. Professors need not reject law school's signature pedagogy, the Socratic Method, but they should contextualize it in law-practice forms and relationships. Professors should show students the meta-cognitive processes (self-evaluating their own learning) that students must acquire. They should also show them how lawyers use those processes to provide legal services, integrating knowledge with skills and ethics. Students should write, advocate, and serve, across the curriculum in simulation pedagogies, including in traditionally doctrinal courses. Law teachers must help students learn with a purpose, in order that law schools not graduate smart people without heart or understanding. The following teaching practices would make learning more explicit than it otherwise might be in traditional law school instruction:

- listing course objectives while explaining how objectives help students focus, prioritize, and learn;

- explaining why you have chosen certain instruction over other forms;

- discussing the challenges students face with certain topics and why;

- sharing empirical data with students on the typical rate of learning;

- openly acknowledging student gains in learning as they occur; and

- reviewing assessments after disclosing results to create a feedback loop for performance improvement.

3) *Reform Assessment.* The Carnegie Foundation's report also emphasized reforming law school assessment. Other professional programs use formative, criterion-referenced assessment. Medical, dental, and other professional-school students face frequent testing closely related to the forms of practice, with intensive feedback designed to help students improve performance. The programs are hard to enter but easier to get out. By contrast, law schools have used primarily or solely summative, norm-referenced grading. Law professors test students infrequently, only for grades, on examinations that are unlike law practice. Students receive little if any useful feedback. Professors do not measure student performance against objective, practice-based criteria but against other students, meaning that some are bound to fail despite the school's assurance on admission that all are qualified for success. Law school is easier to get in but harder to get out. As a result, educators and students know well and document clearly the inordinate stresses of law school.

4) *Focus on Outcomes.* The Carnegie Foundation report also saw the need that law schools focus more on outcomes than inputs, beginning with more clearly defining educational objectives. The challenges law schools face in this area are not entirely their doing. The American Bar Association's Council of the Section on Legal Education and Admissions to the Bar has long been the principal accrediting body for law schools. Unfortunately, unlike the accrediting bodies for other professional schools, the ABA initially wrote accreditation standards to emphasize inputs rather than outcomes. Student-to-faculty ratios, faculty publications, classroom facilities, library titles, study spaces, endowment size, and other resource measures do not necessarily equate to outcomes. Bar-passage rates have been the primary outcome measured for accreditation purposes. Thus, law schools have understandably focused on graduating good test-takers. Yet law practice is much more subtle, rich in skill, and dependent on positive professional ethics and identity than Multistate multiple-choice bar examinations typically measure. The ABA and others have significant work underway to focus more on outcomes relevant to responsible law practice.

Motivation. Any close consideration of how students learn should include reflection on student motivation. Your attitude toward your subject influences student attitudes toward your subject. If you tell them that your subject is hard and boring, then they may feel the same way about it. If instead you show enthusiasm for your exciting and manageable subject, then students may also feel that they can and should learn your subject. In other words, model the behavior that you want to see in students. Yet also design motivating experience. If you design authentic-seeming problems for students to solve using knowledge that you have shown students is relevant to current law issues, then students are more likely to engage your subject fully. The more that you value and reward student autonomy, the more that students are likely to act responsibly. Helping students set their own learning goals further motivates students. Challenging students to learn by showing them the ambiguity and contradictions within their assertions can motivate learning, if your challenges do not demean and instead demonstrate your belief that students can improve their performance.

Avoid thinking of motivation as an invisible reservoir within students, filled or not by circumstances beyond your control, and subject to your modification only by exhorting students to do better. Motivation is not an attribute or characteristic that students either have or do not have no matter your instructional designs or that you can simply exhort into students with frequent admonition. Especially avoid chastising students for apparent lack of motivation. Instead, discern the behaviors that they exhibit that suggest lack of motivation, like coming late to class or web-surfing while in class. Then study your actions that may have discouraged better behavior. If your class is overlong, monotone in delivery, and without relieving breaks to the point of being physically painful and mentally stressful, then more students will come late and leave early, just as they will if your instruction is haphazard, harsh, or demeaning. If instead your class is lively, varied, and well-paced, with appropriate thought to how much students can process and bear, then more students will arrive early, stay late, and fully engage during class time. Take a behavioral approach to student engagement. You are likely more responsible for student motivation than you realize. Dozens of factors affect student motivation, many within your control. Every sound design advocated in this book and elsewhere can contribute to student motivation.

Your greatest achievement may be in helping students adopt a learner's attitude, to become self-regulated learners. Help students see them as you see them, as you evaluate their learning practices. Help students adopt a meta-cognitive stance toward their learning, in which they are reflecting on their own learning practices. Encourage them to self-reflect by journaling on specific learning topics that you suggest to them, like their time management, note-taking practices, planning practices, reading approach, outline organization, and assessment practice. Invite students to share with one another the things that they are learning about their own learning, not just what they are learning about your field and subject. Collect and display student advice on study strategies, study resources, memory work, test-taking strategies, performance reviews, and other learning practices. Pedagogy is not simply about teaching your subject. Pedagogy also includes teaching learning.

Conclusion. You now have a perspective on law school pedagogy. In the end, instruction should help students learn and use the subject matter on the final exam and bar examination, and on the job providing responsible legal services. Your teaching should help law students become skilled, effective, and responsible lawyers. Teaching still has social and communal ends. It also has ends in the individual student's development. Good teachers link instruction to the students' experience and expectations, as well as the interests of the anticipated client, the profession, the community, and the nation. Teaching law is a position of enormous responsibility and opportunity. Respect and enjoy it.

Exercise 1

Try bringing the above theory together in the design of a single class session. Educator Robert Gagne in the classic 1965 text *The Conditions of Learning* wrote that there are nine steps to learning (nine steps to move sensory memory to long-term memory). Thinking of a specific class session, write an instructional plan for each of the following nine steps:

1. Gain students' attention with an interest device connected to the class topic.
2. Alert students to the topic's purpose and significance to help them concentrate and organize thought.

3. Explore students' prior knowledge to help link new learning to existing structures and to help you determine the level of instruction.

4. Present the new information in visible, manageable, and memorable chunks, relevant to the way students will use the information.

5. Provide guidance in incorporating, testing, and organizing the new information, to help students move it to long-term memory.

6. Elicit performances using the new information, to multiply retrieval routes and demonstrate relevancy.

7. Provide feedback assessing the quality of performances against clear criteria, to encourage and support learning.

8. Wrap up with an overall assessment of performance, to confirm long-term memory.

9. Provide summary, review, and outside opportunity for additional practice, to enhance retention.

Chapter 2

Course Objectives

What Students Should Learn

  Introduction. To teach effectively, one should know the purpose for instruction. The idea of rigorous course goals and intermediate learning objectives began in behavioral studies that took place around World War II, addressing the critically important question of how you quickly get an unschooled soldier to be able to perform a complex task in the most challenging of wartime environments. Instruction had to be purposeful, swift, inexpensive, and effective. To make it so, trainers had to define its overarching goals and intermediate objectives against measurable criteria. They also had to determine the conditions (under enemy fire, under water, under sleep deprivation, and so on) under which they expected soldiers to perform and then to train in ways that equipped soldiers to perform under those conditions. Imagine that kind of high-stakes rigor applied to a program of higher education, and you understand better the power and purpose of course goals and learning objectives.

Educators today continue to see course goals and learning objectives as good antidotes in an environment of higher education known more as a rite of passage than for its program goals and accountability. Accrediting bodies, universities, schools, and departments continue to require or urge professors to develop course objectives and to link those objectives to degree-program goals within the school's broad educational mission. Educators hold objectives-writing conferences and workshops. Professional schools were for a time behind this educational curve, isolated from broader university initiatives due to their peculiar mission and staffing. Yet even professional schools have more recently embraced using outcomes measures connected with defined objectives and broader goals. Medical schools, schools of veterinary medicine, dental schools, and engineering schools fundamentally changed their programs, moving away from input measures with summative assessment toward outcomes measures with formative assessment. Law schools lagged in that movement. Yet the American Bar Association's Council of the Section of Legal Education and Admissions to the Bar, which accredits law schools, recently amended its law school accreditation standards to include not only inputs but also outcomes, making critical that law professors understand the place and importance of course objectives.

Advantages. Instructional objectives offer a law professor several advantages. You will find measuring your teaching success to be hard if you have ill-defined objectives. You will not know when you have succeeded if you have not defined clearly what you want students to do. Without objectives, you will also find harder convincing others that you are teaching as the school asked you to do. The school may have chosen the broad course goals in its course description, but the professor must usually define the intermediate learning objectives that will achieve those broad course goals. Objectives help you align your course's instruction to the goals the institution defines in the course description, fitting the course in its place in the curriculum, the school's mission, accreditation requirements, bar-exam preparation, ethics rules, employer demands, agency requirements, and other constituent interests. Course goals allow the law school to demonstrate program accountability to students, accrediting bodies, and other constituents. Objectives promote valid and reliable measurement of student progress toward those goals. In each of these broader ways, course objectives improve teaching.

More specifically, though, proper learning objectives allow you to intelligently choose course content, design and implement cohesive instruction, and objectively measure student performance. They not only help you teach the right things, as the course description defines, but also help you teach those things more effectively. Professors who have learned how to properly write and use learning objectives may discover that for years they have intended content that they never taught, that they taught content that they never assessed, that they assessed content that they never taught, and that they taught and assessed content that they never clearly stated as objectives. Objectives help the professor align instruction and assessment to course goals, so that students learn what the professor desires and demonstrate that learning on appropriate assessment measures.

Objectives do more than help the school and professor. They also help students. Instruction should be transparent. As law changes and lawyers enter new fields, lawyers are necessarily learners. Students benefit by learning explicitly the meta-cognitive (overarching learning) skills that lawyers regularly employ. Objectives help students orient to key concepts and focus their studies. Inviting students to share in the goals of instruction fosters student responsibility, initiative, and engagement. Stating objectives clearly serves to open communication, uniting student and professor. Clearly communicated objectives can increase student motivation and understanding. Objectives can also level the playing field among students of differing entering knowledge and skill. Objectives are a first big step toward addressing law school's unfortunate hide-the-ball, sink-or-swim climate that can frustrate, intimidate, and discourage students.

> *Reflection*
> Imagine yourself a law student again. Which of the following two professors would you prefer?
>
> Professor 1
> You feel as if he teaches whatever he wants to teach.
> You never know what he is going to teach.
> You do not know what he expects from you.
> You do not know what to expect on the final examination.

> Professor 2
> You feel as if she teaches what needs to be taught.
> You always know what she is going to teach.
> You know just what she expects from you.
> You know what to expect on the final examination.
>
> - You can see how students would easily prefer Professor 2 to Professor 1 for the clarity of instructional design and purpose.

Although students may not know the value of well-written objectives, students often intuitively evaluate professors on whether they state, teach, and test relevant knowledge and skills. Students who write on course evaluations that they "had to teach myself" and "never knew what the professor wanted," and that the professor "seemed to jump around a lot," "wasted a lot of time," and "constantly changed subjects," describe failures in teaching that clear objectives could cure. Even in those cases, the instruction may have been well designed, but the students simply did not know its purpose. Connect instruction to learning objectives, and students may understand and accept its forms better, while participating more seriously and effectively in it. Student responsibility for learning begins with the professor's willingness to articulate the learning goals. Students can share in determining educational goals. It may be important to their learning that they do so. But professor and student had better recognize and agree on those goals, or learning may be a substantially greater challenge.

Drafting. Draft learning objectives by first asking what you want students to be able to do by the end of the class. If your course is a doctrinal course, the class-by-class goals may be to be able to recall and apply certain doctrines in certain settings, consistent with certain codes or case law. If your course is a skills or ethics course, class goals may be to be able to exercise specific skills in specific settings to specific criteria established by professional norms and conventions. Once you have discerned the class-level objectives, ask how you will know if students have gotten there. Recognize and state the performance criteria clearly. Then, and only then, ask what instruction you and they need to get them there. Notice how the process of drafting objectives is the reverse of our intuition to begin by deciding on instructional activities and only then consider what learning those activities may produce toward the undefined end. When student and professor read a proper objective, they should each be able to describe the identical performance expected of the student. If they cannot, then the professor needs to rewrite the objective.

A list of learning objectives is not the same as a syllabus outline, although it may be wise to include learning objectives in your syllabus. Syllabi routinely list weekly readings and will often list topics along with those readings. Listing topics is not the same as writing proper learning objectives. A topics list tells students what law subjects are next for study. It does not tell students what you expect them to be able to do after they study the topic, the conditions under which they will have to perform, or the criteria against which you will measure their performance. Students may be able to sense the objectives after having studied each topic on the syllabus. Yet that is precisely the point: students should not have to guess at their learning objectives. You should make objectives available to students before they begin their studies to help them make productive use of study time.

At root, law professors derive objectives from the skills students must acquire to pass the bar examination, gain and hold a job, practice within the customs of the profession, and effectively serve a client within the field of their instruction. You may have other, broader, or more personal goals for students, which is fine if you share them with students. One clinical-law professor would announce to her students that it was her goal to see that none of her students ever worked for a large law firm with corporate clients but instead devoted themselves entirely and forever to serving the poor. Her students would be shot, she would tell them, if she ever found them in a pinstripe suit and wingtip shoes. Her mission may have been consistent or inconsistent with the school's mission, but at least her candor gave students the opportunity to acknowledge and abide by her stated purpose, or drop the course. She may also have found a suitably evocative way of describing the clinic's core service mission. If students did not agree with her stated purpose, then they could choose a different course.

Evocative and personal purposes aside, bar examination, placement, and law practice using the studied subject will ordinarily establish the instructional objectives. You know what these skills are because of your own education, experience, and practice in the field in which you teach. Drafting course objectives can draw more heavily than other course preparation on your knowledge of how lawyers use law knowledge. You must think clearly and deeply of just what lawyers do with what they know. Once you determine the general performances, you can then identify the detailed and discrete knowledge and their associated tasks, like to draft a complaint, prepare a motion and brief, or draft an estate plan, necessary to their accomplishment. You can also arrange individual objectives in the hierarchical order through which students best acquire them.

> *Reflection*
>
> Consider for example the following three objectives. Arrange the objectives in sequential order:
>
> A. Given information on the parenting practices of divorcing parties, apply the custody factors to predict which parent is most likely to receive custody, consistent with the applicable statute, case law, court rules, and local practices.
>
> B. Assuming you are advising a client in a child-custody dispute, name for that client the relevant factors, principles, and procedures for the resolution of that dispute, consistent with the applicable statute, case law, court rules, and local practices.
>
> C. Assuming you represent a client in a child-custody dispute, list the sources for relevant information and how you would obtain that information, consistent with discovery practices and court and ethics rules.
>
> In the above sequence, discovery of the facts would come first (C), followed by discerning and communicating the law (B), and concluded by predicting the probable outcome (A).

Beginning with a rudimentary list of objectives may help you recognize other prime and subsidiary objectives. The bane of instructors is that they will teach with unsatisfactory results ("the students just do not seem to get it") and then teach again with the same unsatisfactory results ("what is wrong with those students") before recognizing untaught subsidiary skills necessary to the performance the instructor seeks. Teach those subsidiary skills, and student performance will undoubtedly improve.

Components. Well-written objectives have three components: (1) the *performance* expected of the student, (2) the *conditions* under which the performance occurs, and (3) the *criteria* for judging the performance. Here are four examples from different courses:

Course	Conditions	Performance	Criteria
Family Law	"Given information on the parenting practices of a divorcing couple … ,"	"… apply the custody factors to predict which parent is most likely to receive custody … ,"	"… consistent with the applicable statute and case law."
Immigration Law	"Given statements of charges against a resident alien … ,"	"… identify which are deportable offenses … ,"	"… consistent with current law, regulation, and agency practice."
Nonprofit Law	"Given descriptions of proposed employment terms and other transactions … ,"	"… identify which would violate the non-distribution constraint for charitable organizations … ,"	"… consistent with IRC 501(c)(3) and interpreting law, rule, and regulation."
Estate Planning	"Given asset lists and proposed estate plans … ,"	"… identify which assets would be included in the probate estate … ,"	"… under EPIC."

The *performance* is the critical part. The performance should begin with a verb describing the student's observable action. The performance does *not* describe what the professor will do (the instruction) but what the student should be able to do (the learned result). Objectives that "the class will discuss," "students will practice," or "the professor will lecture on" the studied subject incorrectly focus on instruction. These objectives fail to identify the purpose of the applied skill or knowledge. If the professor cannot observe the performance that the objective describes, then the professor needs to rewrite the objective. To "understand," "know," and "think" do not state observable performances. They instead describe cognitive states that you cannot directly observe or measure. By contrast, the verbs to "sort," "list," "name," "draft," and "calculate and record" identify observable actions. To "recall and apply" rules, factors, and elements to "predict," "determine," and "advise as to" outcomes also state performances in measurable terms. Column I below lists only unobservable cognitive states. Columns II and III are preferred forms of verbs stating measurable actions.

I	II	III
know	list	organize
comprehend	classify	estimate
understand	name	write
realize	predict	indicate
be able to	choose	differentiate
think	draft	question

Changing your objectives from unobservable states (Column I) to measurable performances (Columns II and III) can lead you to new instructional activities and more productive formative assessment. Once you define in this manner what students must be able to do, the possibilities for explaining, demonstrating, learning, and practicing those performances are more evident. You may find yourself changing all your visual displays, creating new handouts, urging new online exercises, and designing new classroom interactions that encourage and compel students toward the desired performances. You may replace the old urgency of needing to "cover the material" in some vaguely cognitive manner with a new urgency to design instructional forms that get students doing what they need to do to have effectively learned the subject. You can find few more-effective ways to improve your teaching than to write clearly defined objectives for what you propose to teach.

Articulating the *conditions* for performance can be equally fruitful. The conditions describe the environment in, materials with which, or circumstances under which clients expect the lawyer (and you expect the student) to perform. Law practice often begins with the lawyer considering descriptions of events or circumstances of recent happening. Clients describe circumstances and events. Police reports, depositions, complaints, motions and briefs, and other practice materials do likewise. To move forward with drafting, advice, or advocacy, lawyers must first look back for the event or context. Thus, the conditions for performance may often begin with "given description of the circumstances of ..." followed by the subject context such as "a personal injury," "a workplace dispute...," or "a list of creditors...." Clients' factual circumstances in various areas—criminal charges to defend, transactions to negotiate and document, estates to plan—typically determine the conditions for lawyer performances. Objectives do well to refer to those conditions. Describing the conditions under which lawyers must perform helps students understand and prepare for law practice.

Conditions in course objectives, though, are more than a list of client experiences. Lawyers do not analyze their clients' legal needs and events in the abstract. Lawyers practice in their own peculiar professional context. For example, conditions for a tort lawyer's performance may include review of a legal assistant's intake notes, prospective clients consulting the lawyer, insurance claim representatives assigning new files, clients authorizing complaints or third-party complaints, fashioning discovery plans, drafting and responding to summary judgment motions, evaluating settlement offers, choosing trial exhibits, planning the testimony of trial witnesses, and so on. Study the form of the questions on a Multistate Bar Examination or the performance requirements of a Multistate Performance Test, and you will see that the examiners require examinees to contextualize their law knowledge and legal analysis in these and other forms of practice.

> *Reflection*
> Help prepare your students for practice conditions. Make a list of the conditions under which students in your legal field must learn to

> perform, and then state your course objectives in the context of those conditions.

Other common law-practice conditions can include the intake of a new client, the assignment of a case by a managing partner, the review of an existing file, the receipt of discovery responses, counseling a client regarding settlement, arguing a motion, evaluating the opposing side's arguments, preparing for mediation, preparing an opening statement or closing argument, or conducting a jury voir dire. You can use any of these conditions and many others in drafting course objectives identifying for students the conditions under which law firms, clients, and other employers will expect the student to perform. For example, a course objective for early in an environmental-law course may be,

> To prepare for a meeting with a new client facing an environmental issue on the client's lands, identify the materials the client should obtain and bring to the meeting for your review, the information you will need from the client, and the general issues you are most likely to address in that first meeting, consistent with the practices identified in Chapter 1 of your textbook.

Notice that the previous objective ends with a reference to how you will judge student performance. Stating the *criteria* for performance is often the easiest, but still a helpful, part of a well-written objective. Case law, statutes, court rules, ethics rules, and administrative regulations often establish the criteria for a lawyer's performance. Criteria may be as simple as, "…consistent with the wrongful-death act," "…consistent with MCR 2.114," or "…consistent with IRC 501(c)(3)." Policies, procedures, and customs of law firms, corporate-counsel offices, and other institutions where lawyers work establish criteria for other lawyer work. Criteria may state that student performance be consistent with the "management practices of a well-run law firm," "procedures of the public-defender's office," "conventions of corporate counsel," or "agency administrative practices." For example, an immigration law course might state the criteria for determining deportable offenses as established by "the substantive law from the relevant provision of the federal immigration code, any associated regulations, and other administrative manuals and practices." Those who retain, employ, and rely on lawyers, evaluate their performance by diverse criteria. Know those criteria, and express those criteria in your objectives.

> *Reflection*
> Identify specific criteria for a critical performance you expect of students. This practice will help you 1) recognize how you will judge student performance, 2) adapt instruction to promote performances meeting those criteria, and 3) assess performance in a valid and reliable manner. Then write those criteria for your students. Doing so will help students understand your feedback and use feedback they obtain from other sources, to self-monitor their own performance.

Students routinely evaluate law professors against this measure of whether the professor has valid, reliable, transparent, and consistent criteria for their performance. Students might write that a professor "grades harshly," "doesn't tell you what to do until after grading," "never lets you know what to expect," and "is so vague that you never know where you stand." No matter how nuanced the law subject, criteria likely exist against which we expect students to perform. Responsible teaching identifies those criteria.

Course Examples. If you teach a code course, then you will likely base course objectives around the way that practitioners in the field use the code. For example, Rule 1.2(a) of the ABA Model Rules of Professional Conduct, stating "a lawyer shall abide by a client's decisions concerning the objectives of representation…," requires a lawyer to sort the client's lawful objectives from the lawyer's means of achieving those objectives. The related course objective might be, "Given the representation of a new client, identify the client's lawful objectives to which the lawyer must abide as required by Rule 1.2(a)." By contrast, objectives for a claim course, where the student must evaluate the available data against the claim's elements, factors, definitions, and defenses to determine whether the law provides relief, take a different form. A learning objective might be, "Given a corporate client's information regarding a workplace dispute, determine whether the dispute evidences actionable harassment, consistent with federal and state anti-discrimination statutes." Skills courses present another variation, in which students must master a process, such as writing a legal brief or interviewing a client. An objective might be, "After a simulated client interview, the student will identify the client's goals and the estate-planning forms that will meet those goals, consistent with the practices stated at pages 50-60 of the skills manual."

Use. Once you clearly define objectives, you can then design instruction by reducing the objective to its subsidiary tasks. Objectives are at the level of what, in practice, a client might ask a lawyer to do such as "tell me whether I have a claim," "negotiate an acceptable settlement," or "tell me what I may have to pay." The subsidiary tasks are of course more complex. Students accomplish objectives by procedures made up of several discrete and orderly steps. Much of your value as an instructor is discerning those steps through a task analysis, and then showing students the steps that comprise a complete performance. You must also examine the steps for prerequisite skills and knowledge. Professors who for years have taught a frustrating subject with poor results may, by performing a rigorous task analysis, discover that they had incorrectly assumed that students already possessed subordinate skills or knowledge. A task analysis may also help you discover that you are teaching knowledge or skills that students already possess. Students evaluate professors on these measures, writing statements like the professor "teaches over our heads," "assumes that we know what to do," or, conversely, "covered things we learned last term."

Reflection
- Consider a task analysis for the following course objective, listing the subsidiary steps a lawyer would need to know and take to complete the objective:

    Assuming you interview a prospective new client who describes a personal injury during the course of medical treatment, determine and advise as to whether the client has a medical-malpractice claim, consistent with the case law reflected and principles stated in Chapter Eight of the casebook.

- Subsidiary steps may include:

(1) determine when the cause of action arose,

> (2) confirm the applicable limitations period,
>
> (3) identify treating medical-care providers,
>
> (4) obtain appropriate authorizations for release of medical records,
>
> (5) order and confirm receipt of all relevant medical records,
>
> (6) identify and retain qualified experts,
>
> (7) obtain and review qualified opinions from experts,
>
> (8) ensure that the opinions adequately address the standard of care, breach, causation, and damages, and
>
> (9) communicate a qualified opinion to the client.

With a task description complete—with its steps stated, ordered, and categorized, and prerequisites identified—you are ready to choose instruction. If your objective has critical prerequisites, then you may (1) assess the extent to which the students possess them, (2) stimulate their recall, and (3) remediate any absent skill or information. If a task involves the student encoding new information, then you may distribute printed material, deliver lectures, display images, or engage in other encoding support. If the task requires transferring already-acquired skills from another course to your course or from one context within your course to the present context, then you can alert students to those old skills and offer exercises within the new contexts. The effect of instruction using task analyses is to stimulate expectancy, retrieval, perception, encoding, responding, and reinforcement.

Conclusion. When professors write law school course objectives, align them to the bar exam and constituent interests, and implement them through systematic instruction, those practices provide accountability and value in legal education. The overarching goal is professional competence through a planned program of legal instruction. Objectives are a means of achieving that goal. When you articulate proper learning objectives (condition, performance, and criteria), you can align your instruction to the institutional mission, curriculum design, and student capabilities, while designing appropriate instructional activities. You may find teaching more rewarding and satisfying, and your students may find your course more meaningful, valuable, and engaging.

> ***Exercise 2***
> Using the information you learned in this chapter, draft proper objectives for one of the courses you are currently teaching. Be sure that your objectives include the conditions for performance, observable measures for performance, and the criteria against which you will judge performance.

Chapter 3

Syllabi

What to Include and Why

Introduction. To teach effectively, one must organize instruction into a coherent whole. By some means, you must help students connect specific topics to instructional resources and methods (whether readings, classroom activities, online exercises, field work, and so on) toward achieving the course's larger goals. You need to encourage students to recognize and pursue specifically identified objectives, whether fluency in recall and application of certain concepts or mastery of certain professional skills, that together will accomplish the course's larger goals. Students should not experience instruction as a series of unrelated day-to-day activities. You and your students need a pre-determined framework to draw a course's activities together into a comprehensible whole.

Your syllabus plays a critical role in that formidable charge. Professors usually make syllabi available online before the first class and throughout the course. They may also offer them in printed version (hard copy) at the first class. The syllabus is too valuable for students to ignore. Make the syllabus available early and refer to it and rely on it often so that students also do so. Do not depart from the syllabus without announcing that you are doing so in advance to allow time for students to adjust to and prepare for your changes. Justify departures. Do not depart from the syllabus if it will disadvantage students and if you cannot adequately explain your reason for doing so. Consult the academic dean if you are uncertain about a syllabus departure. The law school may require you to submit a syllabus for review and approval, and may also require you to submit any changes. When you do depart from the syllabus, consider amending and republishing it to encourage students to continue to rely on it.

Short Form. Some of us, when new to law teaching, received an exemplar syllabus that lists the professor's name, course name, classroom number, meeting day and time, weekly reading assignments, and maybe contact information and office hours for the professor. The syllabus' role seems to be to getting students to the right classroom at the right time with the right reading material, presuming perhaps that then the magic would happen. One can argue for a short-form syllabus. Short syllabi allow students to discern on their own important aspects about the course, like prerequisites, goals and objectives, professor's qualifications, instructional methods, learning resources, form of assessment, and other helpful information about the purpose and methods of the course and the skills and interests of its designer. If you do not want students to know those attributes of your course in advance, then use a short syllabus that simply lists the class readings and a few other time-and-place details.

Long Form. The long-form syllabus also has much to recommend it as a tool to guide and inform the student. If you assign students 500 pages of reading over the course of the term, you could reasonably consider writing five percent of that amount (about 20 to 25 pages) in a detailed syllabus, thereby preparing students to make the best use of that reading. Think of the efficiencies. For a three-credit course, students are going to spend hour upon hour in class and presumably greater time outside of class preparing, perhaps totaling over 100 hours. In that context, a 20-page syllabus that students can read in just half an hour seems like a reasonable investment of time. Students can copy or cut the weekly reading list out of the long-form syllabus if they wish. You promote student responsibility for learning when you place that list in the context of course goals, learning objectives, and other resources and information. You also help students engage in more productive studies beyond simply reading the assignments.

Although syllabi should reflect various forms, what follows are some of the items that professors commonly include. You may also tell students this information in the first class. Just because it is in your syllabus does not mean that it is off limits for classroom discussion. Yet telling students in class is one thing, while handing it to them in writing and posting it online for reference is another. Both speaking and publishing important and helpful course information are fine, but speaking alone without publishing can leave students without helpful recourse when they are absent. "It's in the syllabus" is an answer that can save you and students much time on unproductive house-keeping questions. Having it in the syllabus can also save potential confusion and embarrassment.

Detail. Many syllabi begin with a caption or cover sheet stating course detail including the course name, section number (no use having a student attend the wrong section of a course), professor's name, classroom number, course day and time, and possibly the final exam day and time if different. Students who attend several classes may appreciate these basic reminders, even if the same information is available in course registration materials or other locations. Students may show up at the wrong location for the wrong class at the wrong time. Help them avoid that waste. So, too, do professors. You may need that reminder of the classroom number or starting time yourself. Putting it on the syllabus cover sheet is a useful convenience. If holidays or your absence are going to require cancellation and rescheduling of a class, then plan and publish the makeup class, including the reserved makeup classroom, in the syllabus before the term.

Curriculum. Syllabi may next describe where the course fits in the curriculum. This description usually includes course prerequisites. In addition to formal prerequisites, the syllabus may also state basic knowledge and skills on which the course will draw, helping students recall that knowledge and activate those skills. For example, skills may include: (i) organizing reading and class notes into frameworks of definitions, rules, and principles; (ii) recalling those definitions, rules, and principles fluently when fact patterns trigger them; and (iii) applying them in analytic order to reach justified conclusions. Including a statement of prerequisite skills can help students gather prior class notes, resources, and outlines that may help them in your course. It may also help students select notebooks, computers, and software, select study partners and groups, and otherwise prepare to exercise those same skills in your course. The syllabus may also include courses that are usually taken at the same time as your course, courses that follow your course, and any degrees, concentrations, awards, or certificates to which taking the course may lead. This information may be available to students in course registration materials, course catalogs, or other locations. Repeating it in the syllabus can reinforce for students how the course contributes to their whole studies.

Listing prerequisites and other curriculum information in your syllabus also helps students trust that you recognize that your course does not exist as an island—that it is one piece of a larger coherent whole. Do you know what other courses your students are taking at the same time as your course? That knowledge may help you coordinate instruction. Students see you as only one of several professors and receive your instruction in the context of other courses, even though you experience your course from a single-instructor perspective. Dissonance between courses can impede learning. Students may lose confidence in the curriculum, professor, and course. A statement or two in your syllabus about how your course is alike and different from other courses students take at the same time can give students confidence in the validity of the whole program and help them understand why you may do things differently than other professors. Ask the associate dean of curriculum to write or review this part of your syllabus. Students will appreciate the comprehensiveness of your view. You may also learn of new opportunities to build on instruction happening simultaneously in your students' other courses.

Goals. Syllabi may state course goals. Broad goals may include bar passage and practice competence in the course subject. Other goals may include improved legal-analysis skills, advocacy or other public speaking, collaboration and teamwork, or research and writing. Stating these goals in the syllabus will help students prepare for and appreciate the purpose of instructional activities. You can also state intermediate objectives. Your syllabus may then guide students to achieve the course's major goals by pursuing the subsidiary learning objectives like those the prior chapter addressed. Listing learning objectives for each class session is another way to help students understand course design, locate and concentrate on helpful course resources, and engage in appropriate study activities.

> *Reflection*
> As you consider the following course goals and learning objectives, think about how they are like or different from lists you would make for your own course:
>
> Course Goals
> Gain competence to practice in the field.
> Acquire knowledge to pass license exams.
> Enhance marketable professional identity.
> Develop positive interpersonal skills.
> Complete coursework for employment.
> Qualify for licensure to practice.
>
> Learning Objectives
> Recognize fact patterns supporting claims.
> Recall and apply elements of claims.
> Analyze disputed claims and defenses.
> Justify conclusions about claims in writing.
> Identify fact sources for investigation.
> Locate sources of controlling authority.

Professor. Students benefit by knowing their professor's qualifications, for the confidence, trust, and reliance that knowledge can engender. Students may overestimate or underestimate a professor's qualifications, each having its own hazards. Professors may have law knowledge and law-practice skills and experience that students have a hard time imagining (just as students often have skills and experiences that professors can hardly imagine). You may take a few minutes of the first class to share your qualifications. Students can benefit by your doing so. On the other hand, some find hard speaking about one's own qualifications without sounding arrogant. Briefly stating in the syllabus, one's relevant experience, resolves that difficulty. The point is not to puff oneself up with importance but to encourage students to rely on you as a guide for learning. Connecting your success with the expectations you have for students is a reliable way of encouraging that trust and reliance. If they so choose, then some of your students will someday be better than you are at your own field. Collectively, they already know more about the world in general than you do. Let them know that you recognize their ability to contribute now and their potential to grow for the future, even as you encourage them to rely on your proven expertise as a practitioner and professor.

> *Reflection*
> Consider listing in your syllabus your top three accomplishments that you would most want students to know, to encourage them to rely on your judgment and practice expertise.

Text. Syllabi, without fail, identify the required texts and weekly readings from those texts. If you do include text and readings, then you will have met student expectations for a syllabus. You can help students further by explaining in the syllabus how lawyers use texts in your field. You can also explain how you intend to use the assigned text in the course and classroom. Students have different ways to read a law text, for instance, in linear fashion (highlighting, making margin notes, and paraphrasing) or analytically (hypothesizing, questioning, skimming ahead for structure, and circling back to confirm). Students also have different purposes for reading a law text, for instance, to find specific authority, develop a general perspective on a new field, or become proficient in a practice area. Help students recognize the purpose of your assigned readings, and help them employ the favored reading methods for meeting those purposes. Consider having your syllabus identify which reading methods you believe will be most fruitful for their studies.

Also, carefully consider your choice of text. Educators do not recognize law school casebooks for their pedagogy-friendly design. Some, and perhaps most, casebooks give little support to students with what educational psychologists might recommend as basic good design. A collection of edited cases and law review articles, plus notes, can provide substantial data and theory but may not provide adequate learning support. Instead, a learning-supportive text might help students identify learning objectives, provide introductory frameworks that help students link new learning to their existing knowledge, provide important practice context, and help students interpret, elaborate, and generate their new learning through case studies, problems, and other interactive applications. Popular law school subjects may have upwards of a dozen different books from which to choose. Many publishers will provide complementary copies for review. Contrast texts. Consult with colleagues who have done the same. You may find texts that are more appropriate.

You may also learn something about your text that you can use to help students. Your syllabus can preview the text for students. Previewing is a valuable teaching technique. State the text's history, explain its structure, and alert students to its biases and gaps. Help students understand and appreciate the skill, experience, and goals of its authors. Setting expectations promotes concentration, understanding, and retention. Explaining the structure of a text can give students a schema around which to construct the desired learning. Consider including in the syllabus other specific guidelines for reading statutes or cases within the text. Doing so can significantly improve students' efficiency in studying and their comprehension and retention of reading assignments.

Policies. Syllabi do not establish school policies. That work is for the student policy manual. Nor do syllabi alter school policies. School policies change by administrative, not individual, action. Syllabi cannot and should not attempt to contradict, interpret, or even supplement school policy. On the other hand, syllabi can establish course requirements the violation of which may result in administrative enforcement of school policies. Indeed, syllabi should list any such course requirements that professors intend to enforce in a way that may require administrative action.

Preparedness requirements are an example. If you require that students write case briefs or answers to assigned problems to bring to class, and you intend to dismiss a student from a class or course for the failure to do so, then the syllabus should list both the requirement and the sanction. If you intend to prohibit students from collaborating on assigned work, and you intend to treat violations of that prohibition as cheating under the Honor Code, then the syllabus should state both the prohibition and the reporting. If you intend to allow students to use certain tools (rulers, compasses) or texts (rulebooks, codebooks) during examinations but prohibit other tools (calculators) or materials (outlines) on penalty of report for cheating, then the syllabus should state the permission, prohibition, and penalty. The school will have established attendance policies. If your method of taking attendance requires student action (sign-in, for instance), then the syllabus should state the action and the consequence of students failing to take it (that the professor will report the student as absent).

Resources. Syllabi can list other resources in addition to the assigned text. Professors and students hold widely differing opinions on the value of these other resources. Identifying them here is not an endorsement. Yet you might consider listing optional texts, statutory supplements, commercial outlines and hornbooks, and law-review articles and abstracts that you or others have written on points of interest within the field. You might also consider listing podcasts of class and review sessions, weblinks, concept maps and outlines that you or others have created, specific illustrations that you have assembled, study sheets that you have created, computer-aided instruction that you have chosen from commercial service providers, past exams and model answers, and practice exams and model answers. Also, consider listing in the syllabus as a resource the weekly class slide shows, handouts, quizzes, study guides, and other instructional tools that you use in the classroom. Doing so can alert and remind students that these materials remain good sources for learning even after their use in the classroom. For any resource you list, include specific information on where to locate or how to access it. Students learn in a variety of ways and through a variety of resources. Only a single student in each term may use some of these resources. That fact should encourage you in, not discourage you from, listing them as resources. Many influences shaped your subject understanding. A syllabus that displays the rich resources within a field gives students similar opportunity.

Methods. You may wish to explain your choice of instructional methods. Students who understand why they are doing what they are doing appreciate and participate better in instructional activities. For instance, much of law's doctrinal knowledge is not particularly useful unless lawyers combine it with the analytic and interpersonal skills that are so much a part of legal services. Some of the best papers and essay answers in doctrinal-course final assessments will display valuable features of professional commitment, personal investment, and even attitudes like interest and compassion. In a doctrinal course, you may require students to participate in frequent breakout groups for role-plays and similar exercises that promote these nuances. Not all students understand the purpose of these activities. Some will see them as unnecessary distractions from the course's core purpose of instilling doctrinal knowledge. If your syllabus explains the value of these methods in developing related affective skills, then you may get greater student engagement in the activities and greater student responsibility for learning valuable nuances. Let your syllabus link instructional activities to professional practices.

> *Reflection*
> Think of an unusual instructional method you employ, the value of which some students might not appreciate. Consider explaining in your next syllabus why you use it, where you have seen it used by others, the studies or theories that support it, and how prior students have validated your use of it.

Paths. The paragraph immediately above suggests that professors compose a course from several intersecting pathways. Your course may have interwoven paths involving substantive law knowledge, analytic skills, practice skills, and professional-attribute development. Knowledge, skills, and ethics are the three dimensions of legal education, present to a degree in every course. Your syllabus can show how you have designed instruction to interweave these three dimensions. For instance, you can list for each week the substantive knowledge, process skill, and identity development then under consideration. While a doctrinal course follows a knowledge path building from one substantive topic to another, it might also follow a skills path across a case or through a complex transaction, and an ethics path highlighting the identity issues that come into play along the way. When students see these paths in the syllabus, they appreciate better the holistic, integrated, sophisticated, and valuable design of your course.

If you are teaching a doctrinal course, then identify a skills vehicle (case or transaction, for instance) to demonstrate and practice how lawyers use your field's doctrine. If you are teaching a skills course, then identify two significant doctrinal fields of law to use as vehicles for the skills. Whether you are teaching a doctrinal or skills course, identify five professional attributes (trust, honesty, competence, diligence, etc.) to emphasize during instruction. Consider how you can describe these other paths in your syllabus so that students develop to a greater degree in the knowledge and practice of your specific field of instruction.

Assessment. Syllabi should detail the form of assessment (paper, mid-term examination, final examination), format of assessment (number of questions, type of questions, time given for questions), and evaluation of assessment (scoring rubric or method and point allocation). Students should have the opportunity to prepare for, practice, and complete assessments. The earlier students know the form, format, and evaluation of assessment, the better they can prepare for and practice them, and complete them successfully. Studies have shown that detailed advance information regarding examinations can reduce deleterious exam anxiety and improve exam performance. Syllabi prepared and available before the course begins are the right time and place for this information. Syllabi can also include information on scoring, including what you value and why. Information on grading must be consistent with school policies. Chapters below on assessment and grading have more information on this subject.

Classroom Technology. Finally, you may wish to include in your syllabus detail about whether you will permit students to audio-record classes, whether you will use presentation equipment, whether you will use sound amplification (microphones), whether students may use laptop computers and, if so, what restrictions you will place on their use (depending on school policies), and other facilities and technology issues. Technology today saturates classrooms. Your choices regarding technology use can have a direct impact on student choices regarding where to sit in the classroom (front or back), what equipment to purchase and use (audio recorders, laptop computers), and how to prepare for and study within the classroom. Your choices may particularly affect students with physical and learning disabilities. Syllabus information can help students better prepare for and adjust to your learning environment.

> *Reflection*
> - Notice how much information of potential significance the syllabus can contain.
> - Think, too, of how many of these matters you routinely state or have intended to state in class.
> - Now estimate the time that it takes to say these things in class, to repeat them in class, and then to answer student questions about them when students have been absent, confused, or not listening.
> - Then think of what valuable instruction you could offer with all that class time given over to substance rather than housekeeping that you could have included in your syllabus.

Conclusion. Professors who have developed and adopted long-form syllabi after having used the short form may notice a marked drop-off in student inquiries on course requirements. They may find that they have fewer mix-ups that require administrative support and clarification. They may also experience relief at not having to spend so much time and energy on matters that are only incidental or are even inconsequential to student learning. Syllabi can be a valuable teaching tool while also freeing you from time and administrative constraints on teaching. Ask around. Examine your own syllabus and the syllabi of others, and design a tool that improves both the teaching and learning experience.

> *Exercise 3*
> Using the long-form syllabus outline described in this chapter, draft or revise and enhance the syllabus for the course you are currently teaching or will be teaching in the upcoming term.

Chapter 4

Lectures

How Students Learn from Them

Introduction. Professors tend to lecture as much or more than they do any other instructional activity. Lectures can have a wide range of effectiveness, depending on their pedagogical form and value. To get the best effects from lecturing, you should know at least a little of what studies show about the various forms and effects of lectures.

> *Reflection*
> What are the purposes and effects of lecturing? How do lectures work?

To better appreciate this inquiry into lecturing, first recognize that lecturing is not a given. Why do we lecture? Lecturing's allure is in part that it makes us feel authoritative, knowledgeable, and safely in control. It is also highly traditional, making lecture the safe thing to do. New professors, especially, lecture, associating the quality of instruction with the quality of a lecture's content and delivery. As lectures taught us, so we teach. Lecturing remains a dominant instructional method in higher education today. It is essentially instructor centered, where the professor is the focal point of and information source for comparatively passive students. Look at your classroom's configuration. Many law schools design classrooms to focus student attention not on other students but on the professor. Institutions give us the title, role, and compensation, and with it the expectation, of professing. Therefore, we lecture.

Yet we need not lecture, as much as it may seem so from the conventions of teaching to the design of the classroom. A professor could (as a well-known saying goes) be a guide on the side rather than sage on the stage. Professors can center instruction not on the professor but on the subject, on the display of image and text, or on students' cognitive, professional, and social development through interactive activities. In the Deweyan view (supported by substantial empirical research), learning occurs through interactive experience saturated in the subject, not through one-way knowledge transfer from lecturing professor to passive students. Students must construct mental imagery that promotes and supports specific actions consistent with the subject's requirements. Look at those large video screens. Look at the eager and ambitious students. Consider the subject itself. Choices fill the classroom. Opportunities abound to do other than lecture. These options force us to examine, justify, and shape lectures. If among all those rich resources we yet choose to make our own talking the center of attention, then we should talk right. If lecture we choose, then we should know why the choice and how best to lecture.

Reflection
- To appreciate how variable the choice to lecture is, try estimating the time you spend on each of the following classroom methods of instruction:

    _____%   Lecture

    _____%   Recitation/Socratic Method

    _____%   Interactive discussion

    _____%   Demonstrations/role-plays

    _____%   Collaborations/group work

    _____%   Guided individual work on problems

> ____%   Students teaching students in pairs
>
> ____%   Guided research and writing
>
> ____%   Video clips
>
> - Now that you have estimated these times, do you think that your allocation is appropriate?
> - How would you consider changing your allocation?
> - Would you consider devoting some time to any of the above activities to which you currently devote no time, in lieu of some lecture?
> - What would be the most appropriate mix of instructional activities for your subject and course objectives?

Cognitive Perspectives. When we lecture, we should do so in the manner students can best learn from lecturing. So how do students learn from lectures? And how can you improve lecturing to serve students better? Cognitive psychology, focusing on the learner's mental processes, provides some hints. Cognitive psychology recognizes that learners must embody meaning, which cannot exist apart from its application through experience—an important premise that tries to knit together a doctrine/practice union that law school unwisely sunders. Cognitive psychology is both a current driving force and bane of educational theory. It is the bane for arguably stripping education of its historical character and identity dimensions, leaving ethical and social crises in schools. Some studies suggest that students today lie, cheat, and steal at historically alarming rates, with bullying, sexual assault, and violence endemic to schools. Although the causes of these conditions are complex, in response educators are once again infusing the curriculum with character and ethics components. Nevertheless, educator interest in cognitive psychology and theory remains strong. Cognitive psychology's study of lecturing shows its better forms and value to educators. Some tendency exists today to denigrate the lecture as an ineffective instructional activity. Yet cognitive psychology suggests that lecturing can still be a useful instructional tool.

> *Reflection*

> - Before you read some of cognitive psychology's suggestions for best learning by lecture, try scoring the following as lecture strengths or weaknesses. As you do so, notice that lectures serve certain pedagogical purposes well and others poorly:
>
> | | | Strong/ | Moderate/ | | | Weak |
> |----|-----------------------------------|---------|-----------|---|---|------|
> | A. | Identifying priority knowledge | 1 | 2 | 3 | 4 | 5 |
> | B. | Constructing knowledge schema | 1 | 2 | 3 | 4 | 5 |
> | C. | Confirming knowledge accuracy | 1 | 2 | 3 | 4 | 5 |
> | D. | Enhancing knowledge structures | 1 | 2 | 3 | 4 | 5 |
> | E. | Assessing knowledge utility | 1 | 2 | 3 | 4 | 5 |
> | F. | Evaluating knowledge concepts | 1 | 2 | 3 | 4 | 5 |
> | G. | Practicing analysis skills | 1 | 2 | 3 | 4 | 5 |
> | H. | Improving communication skills | 1 | 2 | 3 | 4 | 5 |
> | I. | Developing professional identity | 1 | 2 | 3 | 4 | 5 |
>
> - Lecturing's strengths are primarily in the first four knowledge objectives, A, B, C, and D. Other instructional activities may help students more with the remaining objectives E, F, G, H, and I.

According to cognitive-psychology sources like Patricia A. deWinstanley and Robert A. Bjork, *Successful Lecturing: Presenting Information in Ways that Engage Effective Processing*, an effective lecture has several learning functions. Cognitivists relate those functions to the way in which students process stimuli to form persistent knowledge structures (as cognitivists characterize learning). The sound of your voice, sight of your demeanor, and expressed content of your thought affect students in different ways. Primarily, lectures cause students to attend. Students must literally show up for class and then, once there, should (1) pay attention to the lecture. Students should then

(2) interpret what you say, (3) elaborate it, (4) generate it, and (5) retrieve it. Cognitivists give each of these steps a special definition. They also regard each of these steps as distinct and have advice as to how lectures can better support each of them. Consider each step in its turn, from the cognitive psychologist's perspective. You will then better recognize the challenges that law school presents to students and how improved lectures can help them meet those challenges.

Attention. The lecture's first function, gaining student attention, is both obvious but also subtler than you might expect. The lecture should focus student attention on the priority learning. Yet it should do so without dividing attention with dissonant modes and messages. Some ways of gaining attention distract from the subject. Divided attention is detrimental to encoding. The challenge is to focus student attention on the information students must encode rather than to divide or distract that attention with irrelevant images, messages, or stories. You want students to attend to the priority concepts, not to evocative statements that bear no helpful relationship to those concepts. Attention alone is not enough. Students must direct attention to the subject.

> *Reflection*
> - From your most-recent classroom lecturing experiences, contrast an image or story that was distracting (now that you reflect on it) with an image or story that supported and extended the priority information.
> - How can you tell the difference?
> - Do you agree that opportunities exist to reduce dissonance and distraction in your lectures?

Complex, entertaining, but divided and distracting lectures leave students with a false perception of subject familiarity and without the encoding necessary to efficiently retrieve and apply knowledge. The lecture's purpose is not to make students feel good when, instead, they have failed to acquire the necessary information that the lecture intended to convey, in a retrievable and useful form. Watch out for attention-getting methods unrelated to the understanding and structuring of the information. Humor, stories, animations, video clips, and other wake-up calls should not be simply for students to attend to the message. They should carry and advance the message. Given their often abstract, detailed, and textual nature, law studies present special challenges for student attention.

> *Reflection*
> - Consider carefully how the emotive illustrations you use to gain attention support rather than detract from the critical information.
> - Review your lecture notes, or listen to an audio recording of one of your lectures. What opportunities do you see to eliminate distracting attention-getters and replace them with statements that, while appealing stimuli, at the same time advance your pedagogical agenda?

Interpretation. From the student's standpoint, focusing attention on the subject is just the start. Students must then interpret the lecture's information. To *interpret* information carries a special and helpful meaning for educators drawing on cognitive psychology. When students interpret information, they fit the information within their existing knowledge structures, altering those structures to construct new mental imagery. Students do not simply memorize large quantities of unfamiliar material. What they do instead is to integrate or interpret information (including the large quantities of information so typical of law school courses) into already existing cognitive structures, creating new structures from the old. The remarkable discovery here is that *interpretation requires prior knowledge*. Professors do not lecture to tabula-rasa student minds. Indeed, if they try to do so, then they create special and perhaps insurmountable obstacles to student learning. Study has shown that students evaluate professors lower when professors fail to link new learning to existing knowledge structures. Effective lecturing requires linking new information to existing student knowledge in ways that help students construct new mental images. This chapter should be valuable to you if you gain nothing else from reading it than to remember to link new lecture material to existing student knowledge structures.

Examples with which you can help students activate relevant prior knowledge include:

- asking students to think of and share relevant personal experience;
- alerting students to relationships between new and old knowledge;

- linking new material to popular events already known to students;
- illustrating with examples that students likely already know;
- building law scenarios around experiences common to students; and
- using law-scenario figures whose qualities students recognize.

Effective lectures may start with something familiar to students and interweave that familiarity throughout the lecture's introduction of new material. The process is a bit like putting the wallboard, paint, and pictures on the walls of a framed house. You cannot apply the finishes without the frame, which in our analogy is the student's prior knowledge. If you need proof of this interpretation process, then listen carefully to students who speak with you on class breaks or immediately after class while they are still questioning and processing their new knowledge. They often tell you about some personal experience of their own, attempting to connect it with what they just learned. Recognize that students who speak to you in this manner are interpreting the new information in the manner described by cognitive psychologists. Encourage students to do so, not only on breaks but also in and around your lectures. You can design your lectures to include breaks, gaps, triggers, and references that allow students to interpret new information. Given their generally unfamiliar contexts, law studies present special challenges for student interpretation.

> *Reflection*
> Consider carefully how you can activate students' prior knowledge to help them interpret new lecture material. Think of the next complex concept you will teach, and discern a way in which you can help students link it to their existing knowledge structures.

Elaboration. Elaboration is the student's next challenge in listening to your lecture and your next opportunity in lecturing. Once again, you must do more than command the student's attention and help the student interpret the information into existing knowledge structures. Elaboration is the student's next cognitive step toward acquiring useful new knowledge. Elaboration is the cognitive process by which students regenerate the interpreted information in a variety of ways until the student can use the information. The process of elaboration is a bit like looking at an object from several angles to know its features and functions. Students might look at an object once and recognize it as falling within a certain category of objects. Recognition (attention) and categorization (interpretation), though, may not be sufficient for students to understand fully the object's functions and uses. Students need to examine objects of learning through an elaborative process to appreciate their utility.

For example, students may learn the straightforward legal rule that malpractice cases generally require expert testimony. A lecture could readily bring that rule to students' attention and then help them connect the rule to existing knowledge structures, perhaps by reference to other malpractice rules just learned or examples of expert testimony with which students are already familiar. That attention and interpretation, though, would not be sufficient to make the new rule useful in the manner that malpractice cases require. Students must yet elaborate the expert-witness rule. Elaborations of the rule that are critically important to practice in that field include that malpractice cases

- begin only after one has identified and retained qualified experts,

- depend on supportive expert affidavits and testimony from those experts,

- are often dismissed or lost for lack of qualified expert testimony, and

- are made more difficult to prepare and prove, by an unwritten code of silence among expert-witness candidates.

Students who only knew the rule alone would have gained little appreciation for its working. Elaboration increases the information's usefulness. The fascinating corollary is that elaboration also increases the likelihood that student will remember (store long-term) the interpreted information for prompt retrieval. Students who elaborate also remember. Lectures that permit and encourage elaboration help students remember. Cognitive psychologists explain this phenomenon by saying that elaboration increases the number of routes by which the student can retrieve the information. Additional stimuli through elaboration later help trigger the information's retrieval. Think of it as improving issue spotting. Effective lecturing gives students the opportunity to elaborate the information in a variety of different ways. Effective lecturers turn a subject over and over in ways that show its different angles and uses, until students have elaborated the subject into knowledge structures that exam hypotheticals and real professional settings readily trigger.

> *Reflection*
> Think of the last great lecture you heard. It probably had those characteristics. Did the lecture include giving students the opportunity to elaborate in different ways? Name some of those ways.

Generation. Well-crafted lectures can also support the next cognitive step in learning, one that cognitive psychology labels *generation*. Generation is the process by which students reproduce the attended, interpreted, and elaborated information. Generation involves calling back the stored information for further thought. The cognitive effort that generation requires and the facial expressions it produces are among the most interesting aspects of generation. Those blank stares students sometimes give are not necessarily daydreaming. They may instead be productive mulling of concepts to generate greater meaning. Study has shown that professors often misread student expression. Students who nod and smile in constant attendance may be failing to productively interpret, elaborate, and generate information. Professors who urge or require them to do so may be hampering rather than promoting learning. Think of the last time when students seemed, at the height of your lecture, to be oddly blank, perhaps making you think that students were disinterested. They may instead have been thinking deeply to generate the new knowledge. Here lies the value of the pause and silence. When students reassemble and generate encoded learning, they confirm and extend that learning. Generation makes much greater the likelihood that students will effectively learn new information. Lectures that allow, encourage, and even require students to generate information enhance learning.

By contrast, rhetorical questions that the professor quickly answers can inhibit learning, by increasing rather than decreasing the student's passive reliance on the professor's mental activity. Stating a genuine question while giving students ample time to reflect on it can increase active learning. Try this experiment in your next class. Ask aloud a rhetorical question as you might when lecturing, and then resume lecturing as you ordinarily would after having asked that rhetorical question. How long did you wait between question and resuming the lecture? Study has shown average wait times in some settings of just 1.5 seconds. Study has further shown that professors can achieve increased learning (evidenced by more accurate and complex answers) by extending wait time to just three seconds. Giving students more time to generate information, even minutes of time, may be an even more productive strategy. The pregnant pause is a friend, not an enemy, if the pregnancy lasts long enough to produce offspring. Effective lecturing gives students the framework, challenge, and opportunity to generate information. Other instructional activities such as group work and problems can greatly aid generation, but lecturing can also give generation some opportunity.

Retrieval. Finally, retrieval practice also enhances learning. Retrieval is more complex than it sounds. It is the student's cognitive act of locating and calling up previously encoded information in response to a request for relevant use of the information. Retrieval involves bringing forth into expression the right thought to aid the student in performing the task, whether in the classroom, under course examination or bar examination, or after graduation in law practice. Study shows that requiring a student to retrieve encoded information immediately after encoding enhances the ability to retrieve the same information later. So, too, does requiring a student to retrieve the information periodically. Lectures can return several times to the original priority information, each time requiring students to retrieve that information. Professors who practice this technique regularly enhance students' ability to recall the information later.

One might think lecture retrieval opportunities to be limited. Yet lectures can prompt students to engage in call-and-response for immediate retrieval (a highly effective if non-traditional practice in law school classrooms), repeat key information to their neighbors (another effective non-traditional method), retrieve and write down key information minutes later, and return to their lecture notes to periodically relocate and perhaps circle or highlight key information shared earlier. Effective lecturing gives students the opportunity to retrieve recently stored information.

Other Tips. The above five functions form the basic structure that cognitive theory offers for understanding the purpose and benefit of effective lecturing. Following are some other lecturing tips from cognitive theory, again drawn from sources like Patricia A. deWinstanley and Robert A. Bjork, *Successful Lecturing: Presenting Information in Ways that Engage Effective Processing.* Consider the extent to which your lectures incorporate these practices and how you can improve your lectures to do so.

Spacing. Distributing or spacing the information in smaller and more manageable chunks across the lecture (and across the course) with gaps in between helps students to learn new information. Spacing between repetitions of information enables students to perform the elaboration, generation, and retrieval practice in between newly acquired information. An effective lecture does not jam all new information into one segment but instead distributes it across the full lecture with gaps for recovery.

Reflection
- Consider how your lectures space information. Do you chunk information?
- Do you space chunks of information?
- Do you leave gaps between chunked information?

Encoding Variability. A good lecture approaches new information from a variety of perspectives. Using different stimuli and viewpoints allows students to vary the encoding, giving them more opportunities for interpretation, elaboration, and generation, and more routes for retrieval. You can practice variability within a lecture or across the course. For instance, one professor taught the first half of the course (covering all major subjects) out of one book taking a historical and individual approach and then taught the second half of the course (again covering all major subjects) out of a mechanisms-approach book. Even within lectures, variability helps. Consider adding differing perspectives to your lectures.

Providing Structure. Structure within a lecture helps students capture and encode new information. The easiest way is to start with an outline of headings and subheadings. Doing so encourages students to take notes under each heading and subheading. Concept maps are another way. Just using a title or heading between subject areas helps. Students should not be taking notes constantly. Research shows that allowing students to listen for parts of lectures while deferring notes enhances learning. Posting outlines can also relieve students from the perceived need to take constant notes, to allow for more listening. Avoid lecturing in ways that require or encourage students to adopt transcriptionist practices allowing no room for interpretation, elaboration, generation, and retrieval.

> *Reflection*
> - Consider how you are supporting student notes during your lecture. Do your lectures provide students with outline headings and subheading?
> - Do you post outlines and schema so that students can spend more time in class listening and thinking, and less time taking and organizing notes?
> - Do you periodically encourage students to stop taking notes to think more actively about your lecture?

Visual and Mental Imagery. Imagery facilitates learning. The imagery can be pictures, maps, or diagrams. It need not be visual. Mental imagery and mnemonic devices are also valuable. Providing analogies is also helpful. Humor is helpful if it creates a memory device related to learning but not if the humor is unrelated to the subject. Strategic enthusiasm—here and there focused around important topics—is helpful. Constant or absent enthusiasm is not. You should use images and enthusiasm in the middle of lectures where attention wanes. Consider adding imagery to your lectures, choosing appropriate humor, and timing enthusiasm.

Elaborative Interrogation. Certain forms of interrogation work. Simple questions are not particularly helpful. Try *how* and *why* questions requiring students to engage in deep reasoning. These questions help students to elaborate, generate, and retrieve information, enhancing learning. Pose questions based on real events rather than hypothetical questions. Require as many students as possible to attempt to answer. Even just making students predict outcomes helps.

Predictions require a deeper form of reflection on the material than simple content questions or questions answered yes/no.

Reflection
The next time you lecture, listen to your own questions. Classify your questions as shallow or deep. Consider increasing the deep questions and decreasing the shallow questions.

Performance. Finally, there are not only important cognitive but also affective features to effective lecturing. One's voice must be loud enough for all students to hear, even against the backdrop of projector white noise and occasional student chatter. Avoid trailing off at the end of thoughts and mumbling digressions. If the thought is not worth speaking loudly and clearly, then do not say it. Develop a voice that is easy to hear and easy to which to listen, meaning sonorous rather than nasal. Combine rich voice with facial expressions that match, confirm, and elucidate the spoken information. Expressions suggesting surprise, joy, disappointment, anger, and frustration can strengthen the meaning and effect of verbal communication. Make frequent eye contact, while sharing eye contact generously among all students. Moving around the room to speak from different places and angles can help gain and hold student attention. Yet avoid compulsive pacing, distracting hand movements, slouching posture, and dismissive stances and gestures. Relaxed but attentive posture can help students mimic productive attitudes for learning. Also, vary voice and demeanor. Monotone voice and flat affect deprive students of opportunities to attend and confirm their understanding.

Reflection
Consider video recording your lecture and studying it with a trained educator. You may be surprised at how easily you can improve not only the cognitive but also the affective aspects of your lectures.

Conclusion. Enjoy and respect lecturing. It is an immense privilege. Students pay to listen to us talk. Our talk should therefore be prepared and informative. Yet the preparation that effective lecturing takes is not merely preparation on the subject matter of the discipline. Preparation should also focus on the methods, forms, and effects of lecturing. Do not lose the richness and utility of the subject matter to dry, disjointed, rambling, nagging, harsh, and pointless talk. Support student attention, interpretation, elaboration, generation, and retrieval, in the design and execution of your lectures. Leave space for students to interpret, elaborate, and generate new imagery. Recognize and respect the challenges that students face in listening to you speak while attempting to discern, acquire, construct, and use the concepts that they should be learning.

Exercise 4

Design or revise and enhance a lecture for the course you are currently teaching or will be teaching in the upcoming term, using the lecture functions, effects, and tips described in this chapter.

Chapter 5

Socratic Method

Its Most-Effective Uses

Introduction. To teach law effectively, one should know the form and effect of law school's signature pedagogy, the Socratic method. The method certainly has more to it than examining students to determine whether they can recall the content of assignments and embarrassing them when they cannot. When applied improperly, the method can have deep and lasting negative effects. It can divide a learning community between performers and non-performers, winners and losers, successes and failures, and even perpetrators and victims. It can destroy student interest in the subject, disassemble student personality, and disengage students from important ambitions and callings. The method can be a prominently negative aspect of a law school experience that depresses, oppresses, discourages, and distracts students.

Properly employed, the method is much more than an external, fear-driven means to compel students to study harder. The method has deeper and more important purposes, and effects that are more beneficial, than simple motivation. It centers instruction around student inquiry, performance, processing, and affective skills rather than solely on acquiring a static knowledge base. It helps students acquire critical and even fundamental lawyer competencies, including the ability to engage in and express critical thought, represent social issues in an accessible manner, and connect their resolution to principled and historically valued constitutive meanings. Below is more discussion on the method's advantages and disadvantages. But first consider what the method is.

Scholars point out the differences between Socrates' own method and its law school form. Law professors using the method are not gradually challenging student proposition after proposition to dispel students' unsupported premises, while developing student capacity to reason, as Plato represented Socrates as having done. At least, law professors are not exercising that pure of a form of Socrates' art. The *Paper Chase* book, movie, and television show, and other popular representations of law school classrooms, may be only a little more representative of what law professors do in their signature practice. Popular representations have their own distortions.

> *Reflection*
> - What do you remember of your own experience of the Socratic method as a student?
> - What emotions do you remember feeling?
> - What did you think was its purpose?
> - What did you believe was its structure?
> - Were some professors better at it than others were?
> - If so, what made them so?

Components. Consider what the method as law professors practice it is. The Clinical Legal Education Association report *Best Practices for Legal Education* describes the method's law school form as having four steps. In the first step, the professor asks a student to state the case. Stating the case involves elucidating the facts, articulating the rule, and explaining how the facts fit the rule. In the second step, the professor requires the student to relate the case to prior cases. The professor does so by using closed hypotheticals, meaning a hypothetical that has a clear answer that the professor knows and one that the student should also discern from a straightforward application of the rule just drawn from the case. In the third step, the professor employs open hypotheticals that approximate the facts of the case and clearly implicate the rule but have no clear answer and instead draw out the rule's boundaries, ambiguities, and exceptions. This third step requires greater skill both in the choice of open hypotheticals to approximate the facts and implicate the rule and in the professor's parsing of student responses. The professor uses the student's (typically struggling) efforts not to reveal a single right answer (of which none may be) but to encourage policy analysis, narrative development, rule articulation, and textual exegesis. In the fourth and final step, the professor shares from experience lessons about legal procedures and law practice. The method thus concludes with applications of the rule, policies, and strategies, not abstractly but instead set firmly in the context of actual law practice. The method often ends with didactic summary.

For example, you might begin a Socratic examination by simply asking a student, "Please state the case facts and holding," followed by your occasional support and clarification as the student recites. Your next inquiry, the closed hypothetical, might be, "How is the holding of this case consistent or inconsistent with the holding of the prior case?" followed by other questions confirming that the student understands the core aspects of the rule just announced and how the rule confirmed, modified, or extended prior rules on the same subject. Your third inquiry, the open hypothetical, might be, "How should the rule of this case change if the dispute involved family members rather than strangers?" and similar scenarios giving the student the opportunity to explore the rule's purpose, policy, and adaptation. Finally, you might summarize the rule and place it in a practice context with a statement beginning, "Consider now how this holding might influence the practitioner's choice of cases." Notice that these steps move students from recall to understanding, analysis, and application, in successively higher orders of thinking along Bloom's Taxonomy.

The *Best Practices* report felt that this brief, four-step description requires some qualification. For instance, the Socratic method is not its own end. Nor is it an instrument with which to embarrass students while proving one's own intellectual superiority (as the fictional Professor Kingsfield used it). Rather, you should use it only when it is the most efficient and effective method of achieving your specific objectives for that class. Use the method to demonstrate and encourage learning, not to ferret out and reveal the absence of learning. When you do use it, use all four steps in order. Truncating or shuffling the steps of the Method can lead to student frustration and confusion. Do not use the Method reflexively, exclusively, or by default. Think about when and why you are using the method, and use it only when it is the preferred method. You may find the method appropriate for: the beginning, middle, or end of any class, but not throughout the class; for exploring concepts but not introducing or reviewing them; at the beginning and middle of the term but not the end; and when teaching doctrine but not demonstrating skills and modeling ethics. The important thing is to choose its use wisely.

Especially effective professors probably employ Socratic questioning in a more sensitive manner than *Best Practices* depicts. When a student properly articulates the application of a rule to a stated set of facts, professors may use Socratic questioning to lead the student away from that (central) application of the rule and toward the rule's boundary or exceptions. When on the other hand a student improperly articulates the application of a rule to a stated set of facts, has no clear sense of the rule, or is otherwise at a loss, professors may use Socratic questioning to lead the student toward the central, most obvious application of the rule. This sort of questioning back and forth along various spectra is at least one aspect (and perhaps an important value) of Socratic examination when used as an instructional method. It helps the student follow and eventually mimic the professor's mental motions, which should be like the mental processes of judges and lawyers when reasoning.

Attributes. Why use the method? Drawing heavily on recent educational theory, the Carnegie Foundation report *Educating Lawyers* describes certain positive effects of the method. Experts in every field, including law, medicine, nursing, engineering, and theology (the examples used in *Educating Lawyers*) share cognitive skill sets that they adapt to their peculiar professional contexts. The Socratic method is an apprenticeship in the cognitive skill set required of lawyers in their common law-practice settings. The method first requires law students to form relatively simple conceptual models out of highly complex business, social, and family relationships. Doing so requires of the student a critically inductive practice, as they read, winnow, value, choose, and assemble certain facts to the exclusion of others. Their effort produces an extracted model that represents the parties as strategizers. The method then requires students to represent those models in public in order that they can apply rules to them, resulting in conclusions justified by legal analysis. It forces students to see the world through legal categories. In those respects, the method is a tremendously powerful pedagogical tool.

To illustrate this powerful storytelling aspect of the method, choose one or more words from each of the following categories and use those words to tell a story:

- *adjectives* (tall, late, thin, worrisome, annoying, burdensome, harmful);
- *adverbs* (happily, regretfully, carelessly, maliciously, untimely, warily);
- *nouns* (gun, stick, mat, snow, truck, smokestack, rock, headstone);
- *roles* (officer, server, pilot, plumber, operator, chauffeur, friend);
- *relationships* (father, daughter, employer, contractor, wife, neighbor, judge);
- *events* (wedding, injury, professional service, collision, dawn, meeting);
- *settings* (hospital, plant, river, office, residence, neighborhood, corner);
- *anatomy* (arm, leg, head, eye, foot, stomach, elbow, knee, ear, face).

Reflection
- What legal claim does your story support?
- What legal rights does it implicate?
- How would choosing other words telling a different story implicate different legal claims and rights?

Although all those words might have described some aspect of one common story, the criteria under which you selected those words, and the way that you chose to arrange them into fact patterns, was obviously critical to the story you produced. Of course, lawyers do not have nearly such liberty in advocating clients' stories. They do not get to create an imaginary story by picking attractive words off broad lists. Yet lawyers do a lot of picking and choosing from among provable facts. The above exercise suggests the power that lawyers exercise in articulating fact patterns and, as a corollary, the influence the method has in shaping student understanding of client attributes, events, goals, rights, responsibilities, and relationships.

Legal analysis is what lawyers do as a core activity, among many other activities. The method replicates that core practice in a highly abbreviated but still-useful fashion. Legal reasoning provides a deep structure around which lawyers articulate and value their clients' experiences while lawyers bring those experiences into illuminating relationships with society's central principles and meanings. The method allows students to prototype the practice of assembling facts and fitting fact to rule while investigating and confirming the rule's basis. Legal analysis follows a plot. That plot begins with a steady state disrupted by the disputed actions. Lawyers must define those actions in ways that the community accepts as authoritative, to reach resolutions that restore social equilibrium. They do so through language that is at once precise and ambiguous. Precision in the use of terms provides reference points and recognizable structure. Ambiguity in those same terms preserves room to accommodate competing views and interests, and to address human circumstances in all its wondrous (and awful) variety.

Assume, for example, that a student concluded her recitation with the unsupported assertion, "And the defendant obviously acted maliciously." Questions that you might ask the student, to draw out potential uncertainties in the asserted "obviousness" of the defendant's actions, and ambiguities in how the law defines malice, might include:

- "What evidence made the maliciousness of the defendant's actions appear to you to be 'obvious'?"
- "Are there other ways to interpret that evidence?"
- "Name some instances where those same actions might be justified."
- "What evidence would you need to discover to believe that the actions were justified instead of malicious?"

- "What was the relationship of the defendant to the putative victim?"
- "What other relationships might make jurors change their minds about the defendant's alleged maliciousness?"

An effective Socratic examiner could think of other questions that would further encourage the student to reason and justify, while exploring and discerning the rule's principle, effect, fit, purpose, and meaning.

In that sense, the method is essential for students to perfect what on closer inspection looks more like an art than a science. In argument over what constitutes appropriate justice, lawyers employ language nearly as much by art, meaning to project symmetry, balance, and proportion, as by scientific analysis. Lawyers draw clarity out of ambiguity. The method gives you the opportunity to model, and students the opportunity to practice, that complex process. Your feedback coaches students toward mastery of that process, especially as your presence recedes in favor of improved student performance. Your role is not to dominate but to support. You are a guide as students pass through the method's portal. The method's strength is to force students to construct legal meaning. Students know subjects by constructing them. The method's strength is that it demands that students engage in that constructive process.

Faults. Yet not all is well with the method. The cognitive apprenticeship it offers is just one part of a three-fold apprenticeship in knowledge, skills, and ethics, that students need to balance. Therein is one problem. The method's emphasis in first-year courses and throughout the curriculum can produce a crisis in the crucial skills and professional-identity dimensions. The method's acutely analytic and abstract form leaves little room for students to see the human purpose and practical ethics of professional service. Students practicing the method tend to see persons primarily as strategizing parties, when they are instead, foremost, individuals who have multiple valuable social roles like that of employee, volunteer, caretaker, parent, spouse, child, and neighbor. The method and the case opinions on which it depends make complex and uniquely valuable persons into simple and disposable parties, trapped by the narrow legal categories, labels, doctrines, and strategizing actions assigned to them. Students have no clients to serve, even imaginary clients, and so they gain too little sense of a lawyer's responsibility to serve others. Students learn an amoral technical process through which they have little hope of providing satisfying client service or finding satisfying practice meaning. In the method's traditional form, students tend to learn intuitively without recognizing the distinct nature, limited value, and specific purpose of their special form of legal reasoning.

> *Reflection*
> Choose for trial use in your next class one of the following ways in which you might help students to humanize the parties who are the subjects of their recitation. Ask students to:
>
> - use the party's name (Mr. Brown, Ms. Blue) rather than role (plaintiff, defendant);
>
> - articulate other possible motives for the parties' actions than the motives attributed to them in the case opinion;
>
> - conjecture what unknown circumstances might have justified the responsible party's disputed actions;
>
> - infer the quality of the parties' representation from the arguments made by their counsel; and
>
> - estimate the financial, familial, and reputational consequences to the parties if found responsible for everything alleged.
>
> How did your trial effort work? Did you notice any change in student sensitivity to the parties and their positions?

Improvement. You can address these concerns in other ways. First, recognize that a student's entire law school experience, not just the Socratic experience, is in one way or another formative. Learning takes place not just in the method's cognitive apprenticeship but also in skills and ethics, and not only in the classroom but also in various instructional and co- and extra-curricular activities inside and outside the classroom. Help students appreciate and participate in other law school activities outside of the method. Do not allow the method to dominate students' experience to such an extent that students lose sight of the larger goal and other opportunities to achieve it. Help students appreciate that just because they may feel as if they survived or thwarted the method, or succumbed to it, they still have much else to gain from law school. Place the method in its appropriate pedagogical context as an important tool but not the only or even necessarily the central experience of law school.

You can also vary the method to expand the role of skills and ethics. For instance, rather than question students in the abstract, you might consistently assign them roles as representatives of one party or another. Doing so instantly lends practice context. They become the lawyer and you the client, judge, or witness. It also injects into the dialectic the fundamental ethical concept of lawyer responsibility to court, client, opposing party, and witness, and the identity issues surrounding client relationship. It instantly changes the method's abstract quality into something closer to genuine law practice, while removing the student's privilege to speculate without thinking of the personal and professional consequences. It also creates the opportunity for demonstrating counseling and strategic skills. For another instance, you could ask students for competing statements of the case, demonstrating the significance of how different lawyers see, choose, and assemble different stories.

For another example, you might choose for trial use in your next class one of the following ways to help students humanize the parties about whom they recite. Ask students to:

- use the party's name (Mr. Brown, Ms. Blue) rather than role (plaintiff, defendant);

- articulate other possible motives for the parties' actions than the motives attributed to them in the case opinion;

- conjecture what unknown circumstances might have justified the responsible party's disputed actions;

- infer the quality of the parties' representation from the arguments made by their counsel; or

- estimate the financial, familial, and reputational consequences to the parties if found responsible for everything alleged.

These and other modest adaptations can enliven and contextualize the method, especially when its abstract quality has caused its power to wane.

You can also make the method's operation explicit. Tell students what you are doing in using the method and why you are doing it. Explain to them the method's four steps. Show them how you formulate hypotheticals by changing the participants' actions (the *what*), settings (the *where*), and roles (the *who*). Show them how you construct spectra that test the boundaries of the rule. Recognize and congratulate students who intuitively exercise these skills of creating hypotheticals and scales to challenge or support outcomes and rules. Tell them how they just exercised those skills. Doing so equips and empowers students, helping them overcome the fear and passivity, and even the victimization, sometimes associated with the method.

For example, the professor who responds to a student's recital with, "Well, gosh, I never quite know what a student is going to answer when I ask that question," has probably not helped students recognize the method's process and appreciate its value. By contrast, each of the following professor responses would probably help students in both respects:

- "Notice how Mary extended the analogy to ensure that we appreciated its effectiveness."

- "Interesting. You have used a strong contrary example. Can you give us an equally evocative comparative example?"

- "My hypothetical changed the defendant's role and actions, and the setting. Which do you think was the most significant?"

- "Now that we see the rule's core, let's move on to some boundary issues. Does the outcome change if we have no evidence of the defendant's motive?"

You may see significant improvement in student recitation when students understand the method and trust that you also understand it. You will also have shown students not only the specific reasoning skill that they are attempting but also the meta-cognitive processes associated with learning new skills. You can foster in students not just the capacity to reason analytically, analogically, inductively, deductively, and abductively, but to recognize when they are doing so. That extra capacity might help them become masters not just of law but also of learning law, and masters not just of their profession but of their learning and thus of themselves. Making the method transparent frees students to more fully participate in and appreciate the classroom.

In addition, consider differentiating your use of the method to fit the students in the classroom. Some students benefit by more support in reading and comprehension skills. Locating and quoting the relevant language from the case opinion, and having students do so, helps some students recognize the structure and discern the priority content of text. Finding the supporting quote may be overly simple for some students but provide an important link to the text for others. Using examples from the day's news or from student workplaces, rather than hypotheticals set in unfamiliar professional contexts, may help other students anchor their learning. Part-time, working students may respond to different places, events, transactions, news sources, communication devices, cultural icons, and relationships, than full-time non-working students fresh out of undergraduate programs. Know who your students are, and help them draw from their, not merely your, experiences. Students also learn and remember information by evaluating it. Help students reconstitute the case in a sufficiently dramatic narrative that they engage its issue with passion. Students who remain aloof from the narrative lose an opportunity for persistent learning.

For example, depending on the age, experience, residence, and other characteristics of students in your class, you might use either a health club or schoolboard meeting as the setting for a fact pattern. Some students would respond to the health club while having no context for what occurs at a schoolboard meeting. Working students who have children in school may find the schoolboard setting more familiar than the health club. Again, depending on student demographics, you might use either a wedding or starting a business as the event. You might use either purchasing a smartphone or closing on a mortgage as the transaction. You might choose Google or the evening newspaper as the news source. You might choose Twitter or correspondence as the communication device and Eminem or George Harrison as the cultural icon. Hypothetical scenarios might involve relationships based around either school or the workplace. Your choice should draw from context anchored in student experience. Certainly, you can introduce students to unfamiliar practice settings and events. That, too, is part of teaching, including Socratic examination. Yet recognize the value of setting learning in familiar contexts, especially when the challenge is as great as the venerable Socratic method presents. Even Socrates himself frequently gave his students that modest advantage.

Discussion. Some law professors eschew the Socratic professor-as-questioner form in favor of a softer, more-supportive model in which the professor simply leads discussion, eliciting by a combination of observation, direction, and question students' helpful recall, analysis, and evaluation. Effective discussion technique, though, is hardly simple. The professor must involve all students in ways that balance, support, and promote their voluntary participation—no small feat when so-called gunners can dominate discussion and intimidate students who lack the confidence and articulation to consistently participate. These steps can help sustain a positive, participatory discussion environment: be positive rather than critical in your own statements, modeling supportive communication; reframe harsh statements in softer tones and weak statements in stronger terms; allow a few seconds for students to formulate thoughts (silence can be golden); answer a clearly incorrect statement with a guiding question rather than rebuke; show that you, too, are listening to students by highlighting valuable things that students say; keep discussion on topic; require civility of all while being civil yourself; and encourage students to evaluate and respond to one another's statements rather than merely your own.

Help students prepare in advance for discussion, too, using the syllabus to identify discussion topics and pre-class handouts to supply helpful context, guidance, and detail. Articulate discussion rules and protocols in your syllabus or another appropriate referral source. Display those rules and protocols during discussion if discussion has not conformed. Teach students how to engage in discussion in these ways and by modeling sound moderator behavior. Adroitly move the discussion forward across the topic and around the classroom from student to student. Ask questions and give direction to move the discussion from fact construction to law recall to deeper analysis including policy, practical, and pragmatic considerations. Set the discussion in its law-practice context as to how lawyers, clients, judges, witnesses, and others may behave. Use a *parking lot* on the whiteboard to note student comments that, while somewhat off topic, are valuable in other ways and to which you may return later in the discussion or class. Use a back-channel electronic chatroom for students to comment other than orally but only if you are willing to moderate that back-channel for appropriate content.

Conclusion. Legal education, compared to education in other professions, has a unique role in relation to the public. It trains professionals in ways that ensure the proper functioning of indispensable social institutions. Lawyers have an official public role. Law school must therefore be formative of self-reflective and self-directing professionals. The Socratic method has much to do with forming responsible lawyers. Consider carefully some of the above attributes and faults of the method and how to draw on its strengths while remediating its weakness, and you will ensure that it continues to do so.

> ***Exercise 5***
> Using Bloom's Taxonomy of Educational Objectives, create questions that move students from the lower forms of thinking to higher-order thinking for a core concept in the course you are now teaching or planning to teach.

Chapter 6

Differentiating Instruction

How to Serve More Students

Introduction. To teach effectively, one should sufficiently differentiate forms of instruction to reach all learners. Much research exists on the varied learning preferences of undergraduate and graduate students. Examples are the Association for the Study of Higher Education's *Learning Styles: Implications for Improving Educational Practices* and a text co-authored by noted educator Wilbert McKeachie, *Teaching and Learning in the College Classroom—A Review of the Research Literature*. Those and other texts reflect recent recognition of an urgent need to improve teaching in higher education. They also indicate that understanding and accommodating varied learning preferences is critical to that effort.

> *Reflection*
> - Think for a moment of a talent or strength that you displayed as a law student. Did your classmates have that same talent or strength?

- Now think of the academic experience that most helped prepare you for law school. Did your classmates have that same experience?
- Now think of the non-academic experience that most helped prepare you for law school. Notice from this reflection how different your attributes and dispositions were from at least some of your classmates.
- Then here is the hard part: what disposition or attribute did you most need to change to succeed in law school?
- Do you remember what most helped you acquire the new disposition or attribute?

History. Many educators once thought that a student's aptitude for learning was not only the critical variable but also largely beyond the instructor's control. Experiments in the early 1960s tested a variety of teaching techniques under a variety of conditions to show that aptitude was not a major factor in achievement. Educators then developed learning-mastery techniques supporting findings that almost any student can learn. Efforts like these led to a new understanding within higher education. The goal of higher education today is not simply to transfer knowledge from generation to generation but to help individual students equip themselves with the skills and attitudes that will enable them to master and use learning. Effective learning today depends on not only acquiring new knowledge but also identifying learning processes that foster the acquisition of new knowledge. Effective teaching today depends not only on knowledge of the subject matter but also on knowledge of student learning and strategies that motivate students to learn about learning, including learning about cognitive structures, skills, and strategies. Today, instructors bear responsibility for fitting teaching to student learning dispositions, preferences, and practices. Professors today shape learning as much as they shape knowledge.

Reflection
- To demonstrate, try naming three attributes, practices, or dispositions that may affect learning, in which you have seen students differ widely. Given time, you can probably think of many more. Examples may include vocabulary or word comprehension, reading readiness or understanding of text, spelling and grammar, intellectual motivation or interest, concept

> formation, organization skills, and study perseverance or discipline.
> - Notice how students can improve each of these attributes, practices, or dispositions. Probably, you would find it difficult to think of a specific attribute, practice, or disposition that a student could not improve, given time, effort, resources, and your instruction.

Sensitivity. Student learning preferences differ on several measures including personality traits, information-processing habits and speeds, and social-interaction skills. Your sensitivity to those differences makes sense if you want to draw on *and expand* individual student preferences. The pedagogical goal is not merely to match and serve preferences, although doing so can certainly aid learning. The goal also includes helping students build more reliable and productive practices and preferences. Insensitivity to either student preferences *or* student need to build more reliable preferences may increase student attrition. Given the opportunity, students will choose one professor over another for the same course. Why do students professor shop? Many professors would attribute student choice of instructor to grading practices or workload ease. Yet at least some students, and perhaps many, base their choice on instructional format or other characteristics to which they can match their learning practices. Stimulus issues like clarity of voice and visual presentations, resource issues like quantity of online materials and support, organization issues like detail of syllabus and handouts, and diversity issues like sensitivity and openness to culture and view, are all legitimate reasons for students to choose among professors.

Colleges and universities recognize the importance of student preparation, practices, and preferences. To reduce attrition, some institutions match new students who are unprepared for traditional forms of higher-education instruction to professors who possess that sensitivity. The practice is open at some institutions and tacit at others. Parents have always exercised what influence they could to match their children to teachers whom they feel are most appropriate for learning, whether by discipline, depth, sensitivity, or some other measure. Some institutions now do likewise in loco parentis. Institutions that match student to professor early in the curriculum may allow mismatches to occur later, after those students have acquired new study practices. Institutions also hire professors based on sensitivity to learning preferences and willingness to adapt teaching practices.

> *Reflection*
> - Do you recognize your own capacity to learn and change, even as it has to do with teaching?
> - What are your beliefs about teaching style and personality?
> - If you will pardon the expression, do you believe that old dogs can learn new tricks?

Professors can learn and exhibit different teaching preferences, just as students can learn different learning practices. There is no strong reason to believe that professors are any different from students in their capacity to adopt new teaching and learning strategies. Professors do improve teaching over time through reflective practice. Professors whom students initially evaluate as poor instructors can and do improve student evaluations over time to positions of teaching reward and leadership. Other professors remain the same, while still others may decline in perceived teaching skill and performance. Just as true of students, so, too, does your attitude toward your capability to learn and improve go a long way toward determining whether you do so.

Strategies. Learning preferences do not have only to do with external variables like the day, time, and form of instruction. Some of the more fruitful work on learning preferences has been in student cognitive practices. Some students tend to adopt the same learning strategy for learning tasks demanding a variety of strategies. Some students process information reiteratively (using the same strategy repeatedly without accounting for its failure or success), while others have learned to elaborate and diversify their processing strategies. Students who classify, contrast, analyze, and synthesize, learn faster and recall better, and accordingly have higher grade-point averages. Reiterative learners repeat, memorize, and assimilate as given rather than rewording, restating, or rethinking. Your instruction can encourage reiterative learners to develop enhanced learning strategies. When you require elaborative learning, you encourage students to learn and adopt elaborative strategies. Legal education naturally teaches elaborative strategies. Find ways to encourage students to adopt better strategic practices.

> *Reflection*
> - Consider instructional activities that you might try, that would require students to adopt elaborative strategies.
> - For example, as an exercise in classifying, give students a list of potential cases to take on contingency fee, and ask them to sort those they would take from those they would not. Simply reading cases is one thing. Forcing students to classify them as sensible or not sensible demonstrates to students an elaborative learning strategy.
> - As an exercise in contrasting, require students on recitation to state a hypothetical scenario that best illustrates by contrast why the case decision was correct.
> - As an exercise in analysis, give students a list of ten separate sentences, each with just a few spare facts, and ask them to analyze what claim and element each sentence may suggest.
> - As an exercise in synthesizing, ask students to list and then place in logical order the primary concepts of a complex code.

Process. Another way to appreciate differences among students in their cognitive practices is to follow their learning process. Learning involves the four steps of concrete experience, reflective observation, abstract conceptualization, and active experimentation. Students first see or hear stimuli such as the lecture, then think about it, then distill it into recallable concepts, and then actively use those concepts. Students vary in their capacity for and predisposition toward each step of the process. Divergent learners tend toward concrete experience and reflection while convergent learners toward conceptualization and experimentation. Assimilative learners rely on experience and conceptualization, while accommodators rely on experience and experimentation. Some students strategize holistically at the top and work down to the details, while others start with the details and gradually link them together into a whole. Some students prefer to start from a known concept to work toward a new concept (a process called anchoring), while others prefer facts for their own sake and do the linking later. Some students prefer to learn general concepts first, while others prefer to learn factual material first developing the general concepts later.

> *Reflection*

> - For each of the above categories of learners, think of a student whom you are teaching or have taught whose tendencies appeared to fall into the category.
> - As you do so, consider how you could tell which type of learner they best represented.
> - What materials and methods were they using to study?
> - What questions did they ask?
> - Did they give examples, or did they use only the abstract concepts?
> - How did they respond to failures and other challenges?
> - Which students sought out co- and extra-curricular activities where they could experiment with your course's knowledge?
> - Now consider how you could diversify instruction to serve better each of the learners you identified in each category.

Peers. Preferences include not only how professors interact with students but also how students interact with one another. Some students are collaborative learners who benefit more by peer-centered instruction (discussion, small groups), while others are competitive learners who prefer and benefit more by instructor-centered instruction (lecture and Socratic method). Other researchers find students falling into dependent, collaborative, and independent learning categories. Dependent learners benefit by professors lecturing and demonstrating methods, whereas collaborative learners benefit by interacting, questioning, and modeling, and independent learners benefit by facilitation, freedom to act, and requested feedback. Students may also fall into developmental learning-oriented or instrumental grade-oriented categories.

The law school classroom can be a wonderful place for peer-to-peer learning, with your appropriate thought and designs. Request a classroom that has moveable desks, tables, and chairs, rather than the theater-style lecture hall or classroom with fixed seating that only looks forward. Arrange the tables and chairs so that students look toward and interact with one another. Begin group or peer-to-peer work by permitting students to choose groups or partners, which will usually mean the students seated around them. Gradually, encourage or require students to form different groups or pairs. Occasionally, request that a specific student join a different group or partner with a different student, where you see opportunities for student leadership, tutoring, or mentoring. Above all, design specific activities for each group or pair that encourages or requires each student to participate. Articulate different roles, whether lawyer and client, questioner and responder, leader and recorder, or otherwise, so that each student has and must play a role. Show students how the activity relates to the learning objective. Include in the activity a component, usually written, that you can measure to assess whether groups or pairs have accomplished the learning goal. Observe the groups or pairs, guiding, correcting, and encouraging students toward the learning goal. Laud strong group work, encouraging other groups to follow. At the activity's conclusion, have groups or pairs report out to demonstrate their accountability to the class and to share special insights.

Just as students may prefer certain other students or professors, professors may prefer certain kinds of students. A professor who prefers lecturing to other instructional forms might also prefer a student who, among the above measures, is competitive, instructor centered, dependent, and grade oriented. A professor who prefers student-led discussion and role-play may prefer a student who is collaborative, peer centered, independent, and learning oriented.

> *Reflection*
> - If you could choose, what would be the attributes of your model student?
> - Now carefully consider some of the positive attributes of students that you did not include in your preferred model student. Just because students do not match your model, does not mean that they lack valuable learning attributes. Do not fall into the trap of believing that only students who fit your model should receive the full benefit of your instruction. You may have a far greater capacity to adapt than do your students. Given your greater legal knowledge and experience, you very likely do.
> - Because you cannot choose students, how willing are you to modify your preferences to accommodate and include all students?

Modification. Appreciating that students can modify learning preferences is especially important, when one recognizes how important those dispositions are to learning. Student dispositions are, in a sense, their own form of learning intelligence. Dispositions may consist of meta-components like planning and monitoring, performance components used in executing tasks, and strategies to acquire new information. Meta-components include more than planning and monitoring. They also include strategies on what information to store, how to organize it, and what resources to allocate to acquiring it. Students enter law school with differing motivation and personality also affecting their learning ability and styles. Learning personality is not a fixed trait but a process-oriented, dynamic, and teachable characteristic. Motivation is another dynamic factor that, with your help, students can adapt to achieve maximal performance, shifting motivation from short-term extrinsic motivation to longer-term intrinsic motivation based on subject mastery. Students benefit by a moderate level of anxiety rather than low or high anxiety, and with your guidance can adjust accordingly.

Cognitive practice is another dynamic factor your instruction may influence. You can help students modify their cognitive practices by teaching knowledge structures in the context of your substantive instruction. Organizing teaching material, like selecting a well-written course text, can help. Yet teaching students how to organize their learning through concept mapping, networking, schematizing, and related concept structuring can be even more helpful. For instance, offer to hold a student competition in which you collect concept maps from students on a difficult subject in your course. Then choose your top three student works, and have students vote on which is the best of the three. Doing so may generate student interest in and creativity with concept mapping. Be ready to direct students to online or other resources on concept mapping. Also, be ready to illustrate to students how you have seen lawyers use concept mapping to prepare for appellate oral arguments or closing arguments before juries. Some of the best ways to get students to learn and adopt new learning strategies is to show professionals using them.

Metacognition. Again, you may have thought that research on learning preferences and differentiated instruction would center on external variables. Yet notice the significance of differences in student learning strategies like selection, acquisition, construction, and integration. Some educators group learning strategies into cognition, metacognition, and resource management. Cognitive strategies include rehearsal (shadowing, copying, taking notes), elaboration (paraphrasing, summarizing, analogizing, answering questions), and organization (outlining, diagramming). Metacognitive strategies include planning (goal setting, skimming, and generating questions), monitoring (self-testing, attending, and strategizing as to taking tests), and regulating (adjusting reading rate, re-reading, and reviewing). Resource management includes time, study, and effort management, and seeking help from others. Help students broaden and deepen their learning skills using these practices. Model and encourage them in your instruction.

> *Reflection*
> - Consider thinking not to be a talent but a collection of skills.
> - For example, when discussing a problem, show students that they should be able to encode the problem, infer a process for its resolution, compare processes, choose the preferred process, identify rules, and produce the output.
> - Focus on methods and process more than right answers.
> - Integrate thinking-skill instruction into subject material.

Students will recognize and appreciate your efforts. Metacognitive strategies are one of the more productive areas for new instruction. You can offer new activities and resources to improve students' metacognitive practices. In the middle of the term, you could ask each student to list at least one learning goal they have for the remainder of the course, and then collect, list, and organize the goals, distributing them (without individual attribution) to all students. Near the end of one class, you could ask students to skim the reading assigned for the next class and report to a classmate before they leave what they think is the central rule or concept for next week. You could ask every student to bring three questions to the next class, and then in that next class have students exchange questions and discuss answers with a classmate, bringing undecided questions to the whole class' attention for professor support in answering. You could also explain the final exam format to students near the end of the term, and then ask students to identify strategies they intend to use on the exam, listing them on the board. These instructional activities help students acquire strategic learning skills.

Mapping. More deliberate testing and mapping of student preferences can support other learning improvement and teaching reform. One model used to help students acquire massive amounts of information in first-year medical programs (among other educational programs) maps student preferences against symbolic meaning, culture, inferential learning, memory, cognitive practice, teaching preference, and systematic analysis. Testing and mapping help students become independent in their learning by enabling them to recognize their own preferences and then personalize instruction to meet them. Students who receive testing and feedback regarding their individual learning practices tend to earn higher grades. That information can also help professors modify or differentiate instruction. Some institutions publish teaching formats along with course schedules so that students can select an appropriately matched or mismatched teaching form for their own learning (matched early, mismatched later).

Reflection
- Consider writing a brief description of your teaching format that students might use to evaluate whether to take your course or, instead, the same course from another professor.
- Save the description, and return to it from time to time to see how your teaching format has changed and whether you see progress in differentiating instruction.

Instruction. Consider some other specific examples of instruction modified to draw on different student learning preferences. A guided-design course uses problems to help students identify the situation, set the goal, gather information, consider solutions, consider constraints (limiting factors), choose a solution, analyze the solution, produce detail in the solution, and evaluate the solution. Notice that a guided-design course draws on and teaches strategies even as it helps students learn subject content. Students teaching students can also serve well. Study shows that some students teaching in small discussion groups may perform as well as some students taught by professor lecture, while producing superior curiosity and interest. Also, consider constructing learning pairs or cells. Team learning (dividing a class into teams of four to eight students) can work well for certain kinds of learners. If the goal is factual knowledge, then lecture and reading assignments may be preferred. If the goal is retention, thinking, and motivation, then you may prefer less structured methods like discussion, student-led discussion, role-play, skills exercises, and team learning.

Assessment. Learning preferences are also appropriate subjects for classroom assessment. One department that had high student-attrition rates discovered that its members taught in a manner mismatched to the student population. The department readily addressed the mismatch. An astute observer can detect learning preferences by student behavior, eliminating the need for testing. Professors can learn to recognize learning preferences. You can also perform classroom research on how different instructional activities serve different students.

> *Reflection*
> - Try listing instructional formats and resources you have offered or plan to offer in the class that you are teaching now.
> - Distribute the list as a survey near the end the course, asking students to rank each format or resource from 1 (distracting), 2 (not helpful), 3 (neutral), 4 (helpful), to 5 (very helpful).
> - Then consider eliminating, next time you teach the course, any methods that students consistently found to be distracting but preserving all other methods that had at least one adherent who found it helpful or very helpful.
> - Notice how many different formats or resources at least one student finds helpful.
> - Resist eliminating those formats or resources that serve only one or few students, but consider moving them to a forum where students can choose whether to attend or medium they can choose whether to access.

Conclusion. These considerations together suggest that you can and should vary instruction over an individual class and throughout the term. Students occasionally request instructional activities that appear to be directly contradictory and therefore impossible to satisfy. You can satisfy some of those requests by moving one form of instruction to one forum (classroom, online, breakout sessions, written exercises) while offering the contradictory form in another forum. Simply because one student wants more lectures and another less, or one student wants more collaborative learning and another less, does not mean that you cannot serve all students. You can lecture in class, or you can record and podcast lectures for viewing only outside of class. Collaborative activities can take place in class or only in study workshops and breakout sessions. Make effective use of alternative forums, activities, materials, and technologies. You should find that you are able to serve all individual students at their level and within their needs and preferences, to achieve instructional goals.

> *Exercise 6*
> Using what you learned from this chapter, identify three instructional formats that will support student learning, are effective, and are manageable for the content and number of students in the course you are currently teaching or planning to teach, and plan an instructional activity for each of those three formats.

Chapter 7

Integrating Instruction

Joining Knowledge to Skills and Ethics

Introduction. To teach effectively, you should find ways within your instruction to integrate legal education's three dimensions, knowledge, skills, and ethics. Recall that a central theme of the Carnegie Foundation report *Educating Lawyers* was that law schools educate students better when they find ways to bring those three dimensions together. The first year of law school so emphasizes doctrinal knowledge, and law school's signature Socratic method so stresses acontextual reasoning, that students lose important opportunities to develop strong professional skills and healthy professional identity. By contrast, law schools that offer and coordinate multiple integrative strategies, and law professors who support, promote, and draw on those opportunities even in doctrinal instruction, can find those strategies working synergistically to help students form a more balanced, engaged, and effective professional self. Consider integrating knowledge with skills and ethics in your instructional designs.

If you have experience teaching law school, then you can probably identify examples of law students behaving in overly analytical, insufficiently skilled, and insufficiently sensitive manner. You may have read essay answers on final examinations that, though technically correct, are so disappointingly mechanical and sterile that you cannot imagine the students who wrote them serving genuine clients in matters of any consequence. You may have witnessed exchanges between students, in or out of class, that were so focused on technical rights and discrete interests that they completely left out the emotional, identity, social, moral, and political issues that saturate and inform most legal issues. You may have observed students making administrative demands over picayune interests that they ardently represent as important rights, oblivious to their unprofessional tone, institutional reputation, and administrative relationships. Some of these unfortunate behaviors may be due to the heavy influence of law school's overly analytic program.

Even as students engage law school's great doctrinal subjects, they must also learn the practical skills of lawyers and an ethical sense to guide them. One way to accomplish that learning is to integrate the dimensions of legal education from the beginning of law school through its conclusion. Law faculties that restrict skills and ethics instruction to specific courses at isolated points in the curriculum do so at the peril of their students' sound development as ethical practitioners. When and where in its curriculum does your law school teach skills and ethics? How evenly does the curriculum distribute skills and ethics instruction among courses and across the curriculum's duration? Is skills and ethics instruction overly concentrated in single courses in single terms? Where would you find that information?

Curriculum. Institutions develop and maintain curriculum maps to help you understand where your course fits in the institution's overall educational program. Ask for your law school's curriculum map, including especially a map of the knowledge, skills, and ethics that students are learning in courses taught contemporaneously with yours. When the school assigns you a course to teach, ask not only for a course description and pattern syllabus but also for information and documentation on what knowledge, skills, and ethics the curriculum anticipates that the course will address. Communicate, coordinate, and collaborate with professors who are teaching your students during the same term. You will likely find rich opportunities to integrate doctrinal, skills, and ethics instruction.

Subjects. Law schools must balance the integration goal by recognizing the importance of law's doctrinal subjects and the significance of the distinct way in which we teach them. At the same time that it urged law schools to integrate skills and ethics into doctrinal courses, the Carnegie Foundation report *Educating Lawyers* also recognized the value of the Socratic method. Strong programs of legal education will not subjugate to other pedagogical agendas law school's great subjects and the distinct way in which professors teach them. Americans would not be the people they are without covenant (contracts), justice (criminal law), prosperity (property), the Golden Rule (torts), and the embrace of these subjects by the consent of the governed (constitutional law). Integrating these subjects into the practice of law gives the legal profession its purpose and an identity critical to the American experiment.

> *Reflection*
> - Are you aware of any curriculum reforms at other law schools that concern you?
> - What are your concerns?
> - What about those law schools that no longer offer Property, Contracts, Torts, Criminal Law, and Constitutional Law in first-year courses?
> - Do you believe that law schools can teach foundational legal doctrine through a curriculum that offers only problem methods, legal process, comparative law, and practice skills courses?
> - Can you articulate why or why not?
> - Some law schools have made substantial curricular reforms that either eliminate or subordinate traditional first-year doctrinal courses, in favor of problem- and skills-based courses, or international- and comparative-law courses, or both. Who teaches those courses, doctrinal-course professors or skills-course professors? The question should make one wonder how the teaching skills and instructional designs of each type of professor differ and why they differ.

Mixing. How, then, does one integrate skills and ethics into doctrinal courses, while not subordinating profoundly important subjects? Professional schools contextualize knowledge within skills and ethics settings in several ways. One is to mix distinct courses throughout the curriculum, each focusing primarily on only one of the three dimensions, knowledge, skills, or ethics. For example, law students might take research, writing, and ethics courses, along with doctrinal courses, as part of the first-year curriculum. Mixing courses takes no effort on the part of individual professors to integrate skills and ethics instruction into doctrinal courses. From the professors' standpoint, instruction in each of those dimensions remains discrete. The problem for students is that then the dimensions may also remain discrete.

Find out what doctrinal subjects the Professional Responsibility course and skills courses like Research & Writing, Advanced Writing, Pretrial Skills, Trial Skills, and Alternative Dispute Resolution plan to use next term. Are any of them using (teaching) the doctrinal subject that you teach? If so, then what cases and materials are they using? Consider communicating and coordinating with those professors so that their teaching reinforces yours and vice versa. If you are teaching an ethics or skills course, then contact the doctrinal-course professors teaching the same students the same term, to discuss your cases and materials. Doctrinal-course professors may have updated cases and materials that will make your teaching experience more timely and successful. The two of you may also find other ways to draw on and support one another.

Modules. A second way to integrate dimensions of legal education is by module carried across the curriculum. Students who participate in first-year moot-court competition as a co-curricular activity and then organize and lead competitions in the second and third years necessarily integrate knowledge, skills, and ethics within that co-curricular module. Students also integrate program dimensions in other cross-curriculum modules comprised of service learning, law journal service, and student-organization leadership. Law schools institutionalize these co- and extra-curricular activities as sound pedagogical practices, whether required or recommended by accreditation standards or not. Although some of these modules, particularly law journals, are highly traditional law-school activities, they also represent what one educator, Dan Butin in *Service Learning in Higher Education*, calls the *paradigmatic postmodern pedagogy*.

The fully integrative and refreshingly collaborative and purposeful nature of service-learning work, as a prime example, certainly stands to advance the goal of graduating lawyers ready for practice. Study suggests that these kinds of rich learning environments (service learning and team learning on journals and student organizations) can promote intellectual development, work-relevant learning, and enduring learning. Studies show their positive effects on a broad range of measurable student outcomes, particularly in affective attributes like students' sense of capability, awareness of self, awareness of others, and civic engagement, but also classroom engagement. Service learning fulfills both pedagogical imperatives to connect knowledge to practice and epistemological imperatives to prove knowledge as use dependent. Professors can enrich the learning environment with service learning and like opportunities. Professors can connect these experiences to the classroom by introducing students to the opportunities, preparing students for them, creating substantive links of the studied subject to them, and promoting structured opportunities for reflection on how they promote practice preparation.

Like students, professors will find rich inspiration for learning and scholarship in these complex and fluid service-learning environments. Professors must reflect critically and deeply on their subjects to teach well and to produce relevant scholarship. Service environments produce knowledge. They produce the best kind of knowledge in the fastest manner because they promote and require critical reflection on how lawyers use knowledge in the studied field. Think of your own faculty's most relevant publications and your own institution's most relevant innovations, and you may find their origins in service learning of one form or another.

Law schools can also offer portfolio programs to make explicit to students these and other integrative approaches. Students can use their portfolios from the first day to graduation, to see how skills and ethics permeate their studies affecting their future careers. Again, from the professor's standpoint, instruction within each dimension remains discrete. Professors can promote and support student involvement in these modules and become involved themselves. Partnerships with service-learning staff can help professors afford students these complex-learning opportunities, transforming pedagogical practice by connecting doctrinal instruction to students' growing professional identity, as can well-designed centers, initiatives, and programs that facilitate student use of doctrinal knowledge. Professors have several ways to encourage students to integrate course content with other program dimensions.

> *Reflection*
> - Consider how you can better use and promote these modules in your classroom.
> - Investigate and be able to list for students the service-learning opportunities on your law school's campus, through which students might apply your course's skills and doctrinal knowledge. Examples may include volunteer internships at law firms and courts, volunteering at a legal assistance center, accompanying professors and other lawyers on pro-bono service-site visits, supporting local bar association pro-bono committee work, participating in student-organization work on law-related projects, speaking to primary and secondary school classes on law subjects and careers, and assisting professors with writing amicus briefs.
> - Know how to promote these modules in your classroom.
> - Ask students to speak briefly in class about how their experience related to their classroom learning.
> - Mention with praise specific student service-learning work.
> - Allow students to vote on service-learning awards at the end of a course.
> - List service-learning opportunities on visual displays before class, after class, and on class breaks.
> - Invite the school's service-learning staff to speak briefly to the class about opportunities relating to your course's learning.
> - Accompany students to service-learning events.

Courses. The clearest way in which professors can help students integrate dimensions of legal education is to do so within each course. Doctrinal courses like Contracts, Torts, Criminal Law, and Property can include skills and ethics dimensions in which students research, write, plan, resolve, and advocate, and develop and reflect on their emerging professional identity, even while learning the subjects. Saturating doctrinal courses with practical skills and professional identity integrates practice forms, so that the great subjects take authentic rather than abstract shape. Learning to think like a lawyer is alone not enough to make a competent lawyer. Lawyers must integrate skills and ethics into law's large, complex, and profound knowledge base. Lawyers must embed what a lawyer to *knowing* something means, within skilled practice and defined purposes.

> *Reflection*
> - Survey your course now. Can you identify instructional activities that tend to integrate the knowledge, skills, and ethics dimensions of legal education around your course subject?
> - What are those instructional activities?
> - How do they help students integrate program dimensions?
> - You may already be inviting students to do this kind of work but may need to confirm and clarify for students your intention in doing so, in order that they can more fully appreciate their work.

Paths. The chapter on syllabi already suggested that in a doctrinal course, you might require students to participate in frequent breakout groups for role-play and similar exercises that promote these nuances. The same chapter also suggested that you could organize those exercises along interwoven paths involving substantive law knowledge, practice skills, and attribute development. At the same time a doctrinal course follows a knowledge path, building from one substantive topic to another, it might follow a skills path across a case or through a complex transaction, and an ethics path highlighting the identity issues that arise along the way.

> *Reflection*
> - Try making a table of four columns. In the first column, list the number of weeks in your course. In the second column, write the doctrinal topic your course covers for that week. In the third column, list skills you might match with that doctrinal content. In the fourth column, list ethics and identity issues you might address, again matching your doctrinal and skills instruction. At this point, just brainstorm.

> - If you have no clear sense of what to include from outside of your own dimension, consult a colleague who teaches in that area.
> - See if, over the course of a few terms of teaching the course, you can develop clearer, interwoven knowledge, skills, and ethics paths through your course.

Cases. Integrating knowledge into practice is not as hard as it may sound. Law knowledge is already action related. It shapes issues and decisions. Interaction with the environment is the basis of knowledge, meaning not just that knowledge entails mental action but that it also implicates physical activity and social interaction. The common law with which lawyers work is an excellent example of the legal expert's special kind of action knowledge. The common law's wisdom lies more in its action decisions than in its rules justifying those decisions. The common law's authority is not in the rationale used to justify a case decision but in the decision itself. A lawyer's knowledge of law is a lot about the lawyer's knowledge of case decisions, representing actions (not necessarily rules) in certain instances.

You can readily use that action-logic nature of cases to integrate doctrine with skills and ethics during the recitation of cases. For example, you might require students to take specific roles ("If you were the plaintiff's lawyer…," "If you were the defendant…," "If you were a law clerk drafting a bench memorandum…") when discussing a case. You might ask students whether they would take the case on a contingency-fee basis if allowed by the rules of the jurisdiction and then to explain why or why not. You might have students explain the decision to you as if you were the client whose case the students had just lost and challenge students to justify their fees for having pursued the case. You might ask students to explain the case to you as if you were a client in a pending similar case, in which the similarly aligned party had just lost, and you need to know what to do with your case. You might require students to come to the lectern without notes to answer your questions about the case, as if you were the judge and the students the courtroom lawyers. You may prefer any of these methods. Just notice how many ways you have to increase students' sense of the performance and personality nature of doctrinal law knowledge. Can you think of other ways to do so?

Uses. An expert's knowledge is use-dependent. A master cabinetmaker would not tell an apprentice to practice chiseling or hammering until the apprentice *knew* how to do it. The master would instead tell the apprentice to complete a modest cabinet-making project that involved some chiseling or hammering. The knowledge of how to chisel or hammer is integral to the work the apprentice must complete. Children know this truth. If you give one a block of wood on which to practice hammering, then chances are that the useless practice will last barely a minute unless the child can conceive of making something. The worker cannot divorce the hammer's use from that which the hammering creates. Similarly, lawyers possess a special kind of action logic that controls the lawyer's own actions while influencing others. Lawyers do things to know things, just as they know things to do things. One cannot separate doing from knowing or knowing from doing. The relationship between doing and knowing is why lawyers once learned through apprenticeship and why their formal legal education today must (to satisfy accreditation standards) include a clinical component. Law students do not know legal knowledge in the manner that they need to know it until they put it to good use. Only then is it truly the knowledge of a lawyer.

Reflection
- When you make one of the shifts in recitation mentioned above, from non-contextual discussion to practice-context performances, watch carefully the students' first reactions. Even students who have already demonstrated total mastery of the doctrine may initially struggle to employ that doctrine in practice-performance roles.
- Support students' meta-cognitive stance toward their learning with statements like, "Notice how using this law knowledge creates a new cognitive challenge, and so be sure as you study to mentally rehearse these performances." These shifts in perspective to more integrated activities are perfect opportunities for meta-cognitive instruction, to show students clues about the way in which they best think and learn.
- Avoid denigrating students who initially fail while persevering. Avoid statements like, "You thought you knew the material, didn't you?" or "You better study harder next time or you will be

> embarrassed again, won't you?" or "Can anyone do better?" Do not embarrass or discourage students when they encounter new forms of learning.

Conclusion. Education specialist Richard Keeling asserts that students today learn holistically in a transformative process through intertwined experiences inside and outside of the classroom. Knowledge today is abundant, available, and unstable, not a scarce and stable commodity primarily purveyed in classrooms. The primary value of higher education is not to transfer knowledge, which in any case is constantly changing, but to help students acquire the skills and develop the identity to prepare them for life-long learning. In a complex and unstable world economy, adults will continue to return to higher education, higher-education outcomes will change, and expectations for outcomes will increase. The challenge is to conceive of and implement learning structures that integrate learning forms, to help students recognize the relevance of knowledge. Faculty members should make students' reflective processes the core of a newly transformative educational experience. The student's transformation into a reflective, participatory, and effective learner is the broad goal. We must configure new learning processes aimed at identified outcomes. We must create opportunities for students to act on, contemplate, evaluate, and emotionally engage with the knowledge they acquire in traditional classroom forums. Professors must provide opportunities for students to use their knowledge in complex experiences that shape learner identity. In law school, professors do so best when they integrate knowledge with skills and ethics.

> **Exercise 7**
> Identify three key skills embedded in the course you are currently teaching or planning to teach and two ethical attributes critical to practice in that content area. Then plan an instructional activity that will highlight each skill and attribute.

Chapter 8

Classroom Displays

Making Learning Visual

Introduction. To teach effectively, you should appreciate the value of, and either regularly or on occasion use, visual presentations to aid learning. Although they can be of much help, visual displays are neither a must nor panacea. Effective professors employ visual displays to support specific instructional activities, using certain methods and avoiding other pitfalls. Professors should use visuals not reflexively but to help students accomplish specific instructional objectives. Students certainly expect them in many if not most classrooms and often report benefiting from them. Professors, too, rely on them. Give their proper use clear thought.

Forms. A wide variety of presentation media and technologies are available to aid instruction. They include chalkboards and whiteboards, interactive whiteboards, visualizers (overhead projection), slideshows, internet access, YouTube videos, and other audio and video recordings. Higher education has embraced classroom displays of instructional materials. A picture can be worth a thousand words, when the picture has a purpose equivalent to that of the words and the professor employs the picture in a manner that stimulates desired learning. The addition of classroom presentation technology changes instructional opportunities and expectations. Inevitably, whether used or not, technology's availability in the classroom and use by other professors affects your instruction. Classrooms, especially distance-education classrooms, can these days look more like media centers. A professor can take ten to fifteen minutes or more in the classroom just to access and synchronize the technology. Get in the habit of allowing that much or more time in the classroom before the start of your class time. A typical series of steps to get the classroom ready may include the following:

- at a light-switch panel on the wall, dim the lighting at the front of the room for easier screen viewing;

- at the lectern, find and don the wireless microphone after replacing its batteries from a battery charger stored under the lectern;

- turn on the audio system that picks up the wireless microphone and check and adjust the microphone volume;

- turn on the lectern computer and computer screen, and open the slide-show application;

- plug a flash drive into the lectern computer to upload slideshow and word-processing files or access those files from an internet-accessible drive;

- turn on the video player and load or download a video with which to start class;

- turn on the visualizer for text or document display later during class;

- through the lectern computer, access the internet for a YouTube clip and websites on certain persons, entities, events, or sources;

- through the lectern computer, access the course's online forum from which to display course resources and perhaps take an instant electronic poll in class, with students using their laptop computers or smartphones;

- turn on the presentation system that projects the images onto the classroom screens; and

- within the presentation system, choose which media and images to display on which of two classroom screens.

Challenges. The greater challenge to using technology is not technical but pedagogical. Notice how cautiously the introduction qualified the value of visual presentations. You may have heard of studies showing that people remember more when you show and tell them than when you only tell them. Yet simply because a professor represents knowledge visually does not necessarily mean that students will learn more readily. Visual presentations can detract from learning when, for instance, they create distraction and dissonance for students attempting complex processing of auditory stimuli. When students are trying to listen to the professor and other students in interactive discussion to gain the fine points of the law or an argument, visual displays can make that processing much more difficult. Visual displays can also over-simplify complex knowledge, within the confined dimensions of a single slide and the limitations of a professor's graphics capability. They can inculcate student passivity rather than engagement, like watching television rather than engaging in or following closely a vigorous live debate. Visual displays can also dilute priority learning with subsidiary concepts and images.

Visual displays can especially frustrate students who wish to question, think critically, and actively participate. Students will report that professors seem wedded to their slideshows, unwilling to alter their class order to allow for important interaction that could promote better learning. Visual displays can establish an inflexible agenda that deters spontaneity and discourages creativity. None of these problems is entirely necessary; with know-how, you can largely avoid all of them. Yet consider which of these problems you have experienced as a student, professor, or observer. Effective use of visual displays requires careful consideration of their effects and purposes.

Research. Overall, surveys tend to indicate student satisfaction with slideshows and other visual presentations. Students often request them when not offered. However, study shows negative effects when, for instance, a professor reads or paraphrases text simultaneously displayed on the visual. Students may then find it hard either to read or to listen because of the inevitable dissonance between the professor's voice and student's reading. Avoid reading aloud text that you have already displayed on visually. Especially avoid reading aloud with your back turned to the students. Use callouts, highlighting, and motion to call attention to text rather than verbatim reading of it. Ask students to read it to themselves to prepare for discussion. They are already likely doing so.

The same holds true when visual displays contain images that are unrelated to the studied concept. Images can create sensory overload, distraction, and dissonance, thereby impeding student learning. Studies on cognitive load, brain hemisphere function, and interactive learning indicate that specific uses of visual presentations can either detract from or enhance learning. Those studies strongly suggest that you take care in their use. Studies also suggest that overall, visual displays have primarily neutral effects on learning. The rest of this chapter is devoted to encouraging you to further explore, refine, and focus your use of visual presentations. You can eliminate, adopt, or improve visual displays and should do so based on reasonable pedagogical goals.

Reflection
Where among the following four choices do you stand on using visual presentations like slideshows?

A. Have not used and will not ever use them, no matter what.

B. Have used but may decrease use of them, depending.

C. Have used but may increase use of them, depending.

D. Do now and will continue to use them, no matter what.

Goal. The above research suggests that the goals in preparing visual presentations may be to avoid the worst pitfalls, practice the best tendencies, but also carefully consider their uses with specific instructional strategies and course objectives. Do not work make visual presentations an end. Make visual presentations work for you and students. Visuals should remain a means to promote learning on relevant objectives. To encourage you to link your use of visual presentations to specific instructional strategies and course objectives, this chapter organizes discussion of displays around cognitive aspects of learning and helpful principles and illustrations on their use in the classroom. After exploring that theory and suggesting a systematic way to plan the use of visuals, the chapter ends with straightforward do and don't-do lists regarding visual presentations.

Attention. A first legitimate use of visual presentations is to gain student attention. The purpose is not to simply call the class to order through some otherwise meaningless attention grabber. Use visual stimuli to trigger student memories of personal experiences that allow students to anchor new learning. Telling a class that today's subject is *intent* or displaying the word *intent* on a visual slide can be an appropriate transition technique. Instead, though, try a brief video clip that vividly illustrates the maliciousness form of an intentional act. Students may then recall experiences that will allow them to anchor new learning. Doing so also creates context for student learning. Pick a topic with which you feel students have too little experience or connection to readily capture their attention. Then search video sites, and mull your knowledge of film and other video sources, for video that might help the students better acquire the context and engage the concept. Talk with colleagues for other video ideas.

Make viewing experiences active, not passive. If you do use a video clip of anything more than nominal length, then freeze frames for students to share observations and inquiries. Take instant polls, for instance, on whether the actions just depicted create liability of the form students will study in that class session. Avoid interest-capturing sidebars when introducing and exploring essential concepts. Students will remember the sidebar and forget the essential concept. Once you have gained student attention and engagement, turn off visuals. To do so in PowerPoint, for example, hit the *B* key for a black screen or *W* key for white screen until you are ready to reactivate the screen by touching any key.

Organization. You can also use visuals to help students organize concepts. Begin the class by grouping the assigned cases under the concepts you intend the cases to address. Doing so can help students confirm the framework for that class's learning. You can also group and organize fact patterns (perhaps scaling them along their natural continuum), legal rules and concepts (perhaps showing their hierarchical nature), and code sections (perhaps by those that mandate, prohibit, or limit actions). Visual displays can organize more than just course subject matter. Displaying an agenda for the class session can help students attend to and prepare for the coming instruction while appreciating its successive and hierarchical nature. Visual displays can also organize metacognitive strategies by showing how you have linked topics to reading assignments, classroom instructional exercises, and online resources. Avoid allowing visual organization of information to dictate classroom events too rigidly. Be ready to remove the visual display to allow students to reorganize the information in ways meaningful to them.

Reflection
- Examine your latest slideshow, whiteboard notes, or other visual display. Are you simply selecting, shortening, and reproducing bites of information, or are you organizing that information into clearer patterns and frameworks?
- Try organizing better your last visual display.
- Now examine the results of your new effort. Could you remove some information from your organization, giving students the opportunity to complete it?
- Try designing a display that provides students with the components but allows students to organize them. The flexibility of presentation software will often allow you to do both, provide organization and allow students to organize.

Illustration. Most of us probably think first of illustration, when thinking of the potential pedagogical uses of visual presentations. Trial lawyers routinely illustrate for judges and jurors, various events, actions, timelines, documents, damages, and other information. Law professors are more concerned with illustrating legal rules and concepts. Professors should not overlook the value of illustrating their factual and practice contexts, more like trial lawyers. Show photographs and documents (pleadings or accident reports, medical records, and other practice fodder) in visual display. Contextualize instruction in the forms and methods of practice. Display images of the things with which practitioners deal daily.

Reflection

> - As an exercise, think of the three most common pleadings, court papers, forms, reports, or other documents that lawyers practicing in the field in which you teach see day to day in practice. Then plan how you can create or obtain exemplars of each of them to distribute or display in the classroom.
> - How could you incorporate them into an instructional activity helping students learn an important concept in its practice setting?
> - Do not overlook the power of diagrams that illustrate complex events and concepts.
> - Although moving images about the screen of a visual display can easily become distracting, some simpler motions can readily capture changes in events or relationships that students would otherwise find hard to grasp.

Legal concepts that tend to involve three or more differently aligned parties, like security interests (seller, buyer, and lender) and products liability (component-part supplier, manufacturer, distributor, retailer, purchaser, user, and injured party), can require substantial student processing before cognitive structures are solidly in place. Illustrating these concepts can help students build and retain those structures.

For an example of conceptual illustration or modeling, consider the three torts concepts (i) the elements of negligence, (ii) the presumption of negligence arising from violation of statute, and (iii) the definition of proximate cause. The first concept, the elements of negligence, would require only a listing of the elements and may not be the most appropriate for visual depiction. The second concept, how a presumption satisfies the burden of production but not the burdens of proof or pleading, is a complex concept. It could help students for the professor to use simple graphics to show the parties, their evidence, and their burdens changing or remaining the same in the courtroom as their lawyers present evidence of the violation of statute with or without other evidence. The third concept, the definition of proximate cause, is so highly abstract and conceptual that illustration may be less helpful. Illustration could over-simplify what is and perhaps should remain a mystifyingly complex, policy-based concept. Not everything deserves illustration.

Analysis. You can also use visual displays to depict various aspects of legal analysis. You can take a screen shot of the actual code section or case text under consideration, progressively overlaying it with colored boxes with titles showing how the author structured the text. You can reproduce the opening portion of a case opinion and then use callouts to show how an experienced lawyer reads and interprets it. You can display student practice answers to essay questions, using callouts to show how they address or fail to address claims and their elements. You can display portions of a famous case argument, using different-color highlights and title boxes to identify different forms of argument. You can also display only the structure for analysis and not the analysis itself, so that students can use the display as trigger and backdrop for their own oral analysis. Only your imagination limits the ways in which you can visually represent the conceptual motions of experienced lawyers performing legal analysis.

Find a transcript of a favorite lawyer argument, an important passage from a famous case opinion, or a historically critical code section. Format a representative portion of it so that you can get it onto a slide in a readable size. Then experiment with ways to highlight, box, and callout portions of the argument to demonstrate its structure. After using it in class, ask students to do the same with the most-significant text that they will next encounter in your course.

Storage. One of the more interesting uses of visual displays (suggested just above) is to help students store facts and other information while grappling with language and meaning. Consider a typical recitation. The student states case facts and begins to explain the court's application of the legal rule, perhaps relying on a case brief or at least margin notes and highlighted case text. The professor interrupts the student with questions that become increasingly subtler and more complex in the meanings they intend for the student to explore and draw. Students can readily reach the point of conceptual overload, a bit like a computer slowing when it performs too many functions at once. Cognitive studies show that students can process information more readily by storing chunks of it in visual form. Storage is how they use notes, except that when you engage students in colloquy, they must look up at you, losing sight of their notes.

> *Reflection*
> - You can help students store information using slideshows, whiteboards, and other visual displays. Redesign the slide for your course's next major case so that a hidden short statement or simple image crystallizes its basic fact scenario.
> - Then, in class, as soon as the student is finished reciting facts, visually display the short statement or image crystallizing those facts.
> - As soon as the student is finished reciting legal rules, visually display a short phrase crystallizing the rule. The facts and rule are now stored visually, freeing students to process the more searching aspects of your Socratic examination.
> - Notice how students will glance at the visual display to instantly recall facts and rule as they process and articulate deeper applications.

Planning. You should now see the opportunity to use visual presentations to facilitate specific learning goals through specific strategies. How, though, do you systematically plan their use to draw on these several strategies? Consider making a table with columns numbering each class period for a single course's instruction and listing the topics you will cover. Then, make columns for each of the above cognitive strategies attention, organization, illustration, analysis, and synthesis. Then for each class period and topic, brainstorm what visual materials you might use to draw on each of those cognitive strategies. This process will help you systematize your use of visual presentations for the best effects while matching that use to each class period's specific objectives. Your table would also demonstrate your rigorous use of visual presentations to draw on specific cognitive strategies to achieve specific learning objectives.

Conclusion. When you do use visuals, measure their efficacy against the following straightforward do and don't-do lists drawn principally from Professor Deborah Jones Merritt's unpublished research survey *Dodging Bullets: PowerPoint for Law Professors*, summarizing many of the above principles:

DO:
1. Pair visuals with oral discussion.

2. Use visuals to anchor new subjects in prior learning.
3. Personalize oral tone to soften the stiffness of visuals.
4. Use conversational cues to highlight visual details.
5. Use touchstone images summarizing case facts.
6. Use visuals indicating the case's procedural posture.
7. Increase the use of graphics and diagrams.
8. Decrease the use of text.
9. Illustrate transitions.
10. Create visuals leaving out detail for students to complete.
11. Use paper handouts promoting interaction with text.
12. Link visuals with paper handouts.
13. Simplify visuals using few colors and solid background.
14. Use a single background throughout a single presentation.
15. Continue to interact informally with students.
16. Turn off visuals to increase informal interaction.
17. Maintain eye contact with students.
18. Use slides that interact with the text and images.
19. Use a single font without finishing strokes or feet.

DO NOT:
1. Place large quantities of text on visuals.
2. Read aloud visualized text.
3. Use annoying sounds and distracting motions.
4. Formalize discussion to match formal visuals.
5. Clutter visuals with distracting images.
6. Increase the use of text.
7. Decrease the use of graphics and diagrams.
8. Use perfect visuals leaving nothing to complete.
9. Cease using paper handouts.
10. Complicate visuals with colors and patterned background.
11. Use multiple layouts and styles in a single presentation.
12. Use interest-grabbing sidebars.

13. Allow visuals to reduce informal interaction.
14. Display visuals before, throughout, and after class.
15. Look at visuals or computer screen rather than students.
16. Use logos and embellishments on every slide.
17. Use multiple fonts with fancy strokes.

Exercise 8
Identify a critical complex concept in the next class session you will teach. Then design a visual display (flowchart, diagram, analogy, cartoon, prop, etc.) that will help students understand, interpret, elaborate, generate, and apply that concept.

Chapter 9

Inclusion

Sustaining an Inclusive Environment

Introduction. To teach effectively, one must reflect and promote intercultural skills among diverse students. Professors teach diverse students, who live and will someday practice within diverse communities. The year 2000 United States census identified one-third of the nation's population as minority, with Hispanic and Latino Americans at 13% of the population, African Americans at 12%, and significant percentages of Asian Americans, Native Americans, Alaska Natives, and Pacific Islanders. Minority populations will continue to grow. This trend will continue to affect the provision of legal services and the training of lawyers. Professionals need strong intercultural skills. Instruction in intercultural skills is an increasing component of education at all levels including professional education. Many professors have had diversity training or can name texts that have influenced their understanding of intercultural matters. Intercultural skills are increasingly commonplace and a necessity.

Experience. To more fully appreciate the challenges and opportunities that diversity initiatives on campus present, and the perspective you may wish to adopt on them, consider first some history and then the prevailing model. Diversity instruction once stressed membership in differently defined and situated groups. Schools continue to reflect multicultural approaches in such common campus activities as diversity-day or culture-week events, student organizations based on sex, ethnicity, or similar characteristic or affinity, and library displays celebrating minority figures and groups. Multicultural approaches support students who benefit from group identity. Multicultural instruction can increase perpetrator-victim and blame-shame behaviors between individual members of different groups. These binary conflicts can detract from, rather than contribute to, supportive and collaborative learning environments. Multicultural initiatives emphasizing group ethnic identities can also diminish opportunities to build individual identity both within and outside of the identified group.

These unintended effects can increase alienation for those students who had not already constructed positive ethnic identities from their families, circumstances, or experiences. Study suggests that non-minority students who possess strong ethnic identities are more likely to participate positively in a diverse campus community. Individuals who feel that they have no ethnic or cultural identity may fail to appreciate the ethnic and cultural context through which they view events and relationships.

> *Reflection*
> - Help students recognize and value their own ethnic and cultural identities, even while you learn more about your own.
> - Be able to identify the aspects of your ethnic and cultural identity that you regard as either positive or negative, particularly including whether you consider them assets or obstacles to your teaching and other professional service.

Reform. Diversity instruction then moved to structural critiques of systems and institutions. Committed scholars promulgated a substantial body of critical literature that continues to contribute to important understandings. Examples of critical approaches to diversity education include symposia on access to justice, panel events addressing the minority pipeline to the profession, and law-review articles on racial trends in law school admissions. Yet this approach can alienate students from important means by which those students might most usefully bring about change. Standing outside power structures while condemning them may not be the most productive means for positive influence and change, especially when those reforms require the exercise of power. Critical approaches also may work better for professors who have substantial liberty in their leadership roles than for students whose liberties families, finances, and future workplaces may constrain. Consider your view of the structural causes for discrimination. How might that view unintentionally influence students to participate or not participate in activities that qualify them for positions of power and influence?

Today. Diversity instruction may presently trend toward inter-subjective approaches. Everyone, not just members of certain groups, has a story, the knowledge and telling of which can both build community and be individually cathartic. Individuals can express their own history and individuality to other individuals within safe communities of supportive listeners, without making other cultures the grist for their own identity. Another healthy aspect to this shift in perspectives is that it requires complementary speakers and listeners frequently exchanging roles, fostering supportive relationship and dialogue rather than one-sided shouting. A more responsible and participatory democracy results when individuals help each other develop more positive and responsible identities.

> *Reflection*
> - Think of a recent time when you listened to a student's story and realized that they were grappling with their sense of personal identity in an unfamiliar professional environment. How did you support their exploration?
> - Were you able to share with them something encouraging about how professional education and work reshaped your own personal identity?

You can design instructional activities within your course that enable individual students to draw on significant aspects of their personal experience and identity while accomplishing professional tasks. An example might be to ask students in an introductory session to a contract-law class to split up into pairs. Then ask students to assign attorney and client roles within each pair. Then have the attorney interview the client about an instance when the client felt cheated out of a bargained-for benefit because of differences between the client's sex, ethnicity, experience, or other identity and that of the person with whom they were dealing. Lawyers often find legal issues embedded in issues of social perspective, cultural experience, and ethnic identity. Help students recognize the sensitivity, complexity, and power of these issues as they affect legal rights and interests.

Responsibility. Both undergraduate and professional programs instruct in diversity and cultural competence, using abundant resources. Both minority and non-minority students appreciate appropriately designed diversity instruction. Study shows that students value the diversity of their educational institutions and their institutions' commitment to diversity. While students often report satisfaction with their diversity instruction, study also shows that after graduation many report that their campus diversity experience was inadequate for the workplace. Such is the state of globalizing economies and demographics that students and graduates experience ever-greater diversity. Cultural competency is especially important to the legal profession, with its harmonizing ideals. Lawyers cannot ignore cultural competency, with an increasingly diverse potential client base. Law schools should play an integral role in the development of cultural competency in their students.

Reflection
- Recall your own role in the profession. How does your skill at understanding and affording respect to others who are drawing on experiences different from your own affect your ability to perform as a professional?
- Are you skilled at inter-cultural interaction?
- Can you recall a professional who was not skilled and the concomitant effect on that professional's reputation and legal services?

Depending on the student demographic, a substantial probability may exist that law school graduates will encounter greater diversity in the workplace than they did in the law school classroom and campus. Think of the diversity a lawyer might encounter in each of the following workplaces:

(1) in the corporate counsel's office of a Fortune 100 company;
(2) in management at a global legal outsourcing firm;
(3) at a store-front, general-practice law firm in an urban area;
(4) in a mid-size civil-litigation firm in a metropolitan area;
(5) as a family-court referee in a county in a coastal state;
(6) as legal-services lawyer in a southern border city;
(7) in a public defender's office having more than 10 employees.

You probably now have a clearer sense of students' inter-cultural challenges and the competence they must possess. Law schools need to prepare graduates for these workplaces.

Model. To support student development of intercultural professional skills, professors would benefit by a conceptual model consistent with the current inter-subjective approaches. Former multicultural approaches might have had professionals learn more about group characteristics to be able to attribute preferences when providing service to their individual members. Nevertheless, attribution can too easily become inappropriate discrimination depending on how, what, and the skill with which a lawyer attributes. Category-based attribution requires knowing reliable detail about the categories, correctly discerning membership in the category, and correctly discerning that the individual possesses the category-based attribute. The large and growing number of ethnic categories, their constantly varying characteristics, and the individual variations and anomalies within those categories combine to create substantial room for error. Yet a professional must minimize errors relating to cultural issues, to sustain professional relationships of trust and integrity in highly charged legal settings.

Observation-based attribution eliminates these hazards while increasing a lawyer's sensitivity to client attributes and preferences. To avoid inappropriate discrimination, professionals should attribute by observation more so than by class, category, or group characteristic. To discern relevant capacities, preferences, needs, and interests, lawyers should take clues from what clients and others express and the way in which they express it.

Reflection

> - Think of an instance when acting as a lawyer, it became embarrassingly apparent to a client or other person with whom you were dealing that you had incorrectly assumed something about their interest, experience, orientation, preferences, lifestyle, activities, proclivities, or other identity issue. Consider how your error affected your ability to serve.
> - Also, consider whether students would learn by hearing about your misstep.

Framework. To be skilled in observation-based attribution, lawyers need a conceptual framework for attribution, awareness of their own attributes within that framework, and skill in applying the framework in a way that contributes to the professional service. Attributions should be value-free, relevant, and detailed. Value-free attributes likely to be relevant to professional service include the following:

(1) communication preferences, whether intimate, casual, consultative, formal, or frozen;

(2) cognitive habits in objective-setting, planning, implementing, and assessing;

(3) reference systems, whether therapeutic, providential, probabilistic, moral, spiritual, instrumental, or pragmatic;

(4) resources, including food, housing, transportation, time, and legal status; and

(5) relationship preferences, whether transactional, relational, expert, or non-expert.

These attributes provide professionals with a framework within which to better understand and serve diverse clients. The instructional challenge is twofold: (1) to treat students in ways that gain and hold their trust and respect; and (2) to help students learn to treat others in the same manner.

> *Reflection*
> - Think for a moment of a former client. Try classifying that client in each of the five above categories.
> - Did they prefer to communicate in casual or formal manner, or some other manner?

> - How skilled were they with the listed cognitive habits?
> - What was their reference system?
> - How were their resources limited?
> - How did they prefer to structure their relationship with you?
> - Notice how the framework calls your attention to client attributes that might help you understand and serve them better.
> - Now think for a moment of a present or former student. Do you see how they, like clients, can also differ on each of the five above measures and how you might be able to adapt instructional relationships, resources, and activities to serve the student better?

Classroom. Attribute categories do not alone define an institution's culture. The quality of interpersonal interactions defines an institution's culture, measured within the above framework. A law school can have higher or lower percentages of various minority students and still have either a more sensitive and supportive, or a less sensitive and supportive, environment. The quality of your classroom environment will depend on your willingness and ability to adapt your communication styles, cognitive practices, references, resource demands, and relationship preferences to those of individual students, and to help students do so among one another. If you model and instruct in these intercultural skills, then you will sustain and improve a supportive and collaborative learning environment for all students. If you do not, then more likely, students will find the environment non-supportive and will contribute to its negative nature. Do not underestimate your influence on the campus's cultural environment.

Following is a list of specific principles guiding your classroom support of diversity, drawn from Helen Fox's *"When Race Breaks Out"—Conversations About Race and Racism in College Classrooms.* The list paraphrases the principles and supplies the examples:

- **Model sensitive inter-cultural interaction**

    Yes: "Would you please help me pronounce your name correctly? I want to get it right."

    No: "I'll never get your name right. I'll just call you 'Joe.'"

- **Appreciate student needs for respect**

Yes: "I am stopping the discussion for each of us to reflect. We want no one to be hurt by it."

No: "Go ahead and say what you want to say. Other students need to 'toughen up.'"

- **Affirm similarities**

    Yes: "If we each thought about it, we might recall a similar experience of our own."

    No: "I've never heard of that. Where do you get this stuff?"

- **Show that all students can trust you**

    Yes: "Please let us hear your evaluation. Sometimes we speak to discern."

    No: "Now look, I don't want some kook telling us things we don't need to hear."

- **Avoid asking students to speak for their ethnic group**

    Yes: "We each have our own experiences. What is your personal understanding?"

    No: "How would your people—I mean, uh, people of your ancestry—feel about that?"

- **Allow students to exhibit and explore ethnic identities**

    Yes: "I appreciate your willingness to connect your conclusion with an ethnic identity."

    No: "We're not going to get into that here. We check our ethnicity at the door."

- **Promote dialogue about race, racism, and privilege**

    Yes: "Think of the privileges the problem assumes. Would everyone have that opportunity?"

    No: "Let's stay away from that. This is not an Encounter with Cultures class."

- **Encourage students to move beyond silence and superficiality**

Yes: "That sounds simple. Do you think it reflects the client's personal experience?"

No: "The law treats us as equals, and we'll leave it at that."

- **Promote discussion of studies, literature, and texts**

    Yes: "Anyone who knows of something helpful on this subject, email me, and I will post the citation."

    No: "I have never heard of that and am not much interested in it. Let's move on."

- **Help students recognize intercultural insensitivity**

    Yes: "Let's stop for a moment. Do you think someone could take what you said the wrong way?"

    No: "Everyone has their own view. I don't see anything wrong with expressing it."

- **Help students develop reasons against insensitivity**

    Yes: "What do you think would be the effect of an insensitive statement in this situation?"

    No: "Go figure. I have no idea what happened and don't much care."

- **Counsel frustrated, angry, and resistant students**

    Yes: "Why don't you come see me after class, if you have a few minutes, so we can chat?"

    No: "Look, that's your problem, not mine, if you can't handle it."

- **Start with students where they are**

    Yes: "At that moment, are you thinking about keeping your job? Let's start with that."

    No: "Forget about your problems. What is the judge supposed to do?"

- **Be aware of your own ethnic identity**

    Yes: "My grandmother was an Ellis Islander like the plaintiff—fearful and confused, she said."

No: "I guess I am just a good-old, red-blooded American. I don't get the point."

- **Recognize contributions of ethnic-majority students**

    Yes: "We should appreciate your classmate's sensitivity for the defendant's perspective."

    No: "After all, what do you have to say about that issue, without any such experience of your own?"

Conclusion. Notice how learning links success in modeling intercultural competence to the attitudes and performances required for learning in general. You must maintain sensitivity, humility, and the confidence to explore, if you are to be skilled in intercultural competence, just as you must if you are to be skilled in teaching and learning. You should adopt, maintain, develop, and promote a conceptual framework that you and others have subjected to critical scrutiny. Perhaps above all, when facing issues of diversity, get colleagues' and administrators' advice, and use the abundant research resources. Do not struggle forward alone. On these issues, you will find wisdom through the counsel of many.

Exercise 9

Using the diversity principles and examples outlined in this chapter, plan an instructional activity to use in the course you are currently teaching or planning to teach, that will enhance your course's inclusive environment.

Chapter 10

Assessment

Creating Student Feedback Loops

Introduction. To teach effectively, you must assess students consistent with accepted assessment principles and methodologies, for the proper purposes of assessment. This chapter addresses the purpose of assessment including its basis, validity, reliability, fairness, and forms. Following chapters address how to draft, score, and grade specific forms of summative assessment. This chapter draws from Michael Josephson's 701-page, two-volume study *Learning & Evaluation in Law School* presented to the American Association of Law Schools and from other sources. Professor Josephson and others have used rigorous psychometric principles to evaluate, critique, and guide law-school assessment. Assessment in education, including institutional, curricular, teaching, and classroom assessment, is a fascinating, complex, and powerful subject. This chapter addresses only a narrow, but still practical and important, aspect of assessment. It also focuses on traditional forms of law school assessment because of their prevalence. Non-traditional forms of assessment, like portfolios and peer review, can also help students greatly.

> *Reflection*
> - While reading this chapter, it may help you to think about your own student experience with law school assessment. What forms of assessment did your law professors use?
> - Which forms seemed to you to be most fair, helpful, and appropriate?
> - What feedback (other than grades) did you receive?
> - What difference did the feedback make to you in your studies?
> - Do you feel that the way in which your professors used assessment when you were in law school was valid, reliable, and fair?
> - Did it accurately measure your performance relative to important professional standards?
>
> Your answers to these questions may encourage you to consider more carefully your own assessment practices.

Formative Assessment. As suggested above, assessment has both formative and summative purposes. Consider formative assessment. Assessment should, by what we know as the *feedback loop*, play a significant role in helping students gauge their learning to alter and improve study habits. Assessment is not solely to grade, rank, and winnow students. Professors also employ assessment to help students learn. Students benefit by knowing their level of performance far in advance of the final exam, to provide them additional opportunity to practice and improve. Final exam results should not be a surprise. Formative assessment works hand in hand with summative assessment. Students should be able to judge formatively their progress toward the final summative assessment, so that they can make appropriate adjustments in their study practices and test performances along the way.

You have plenty of opportunity to provide students with formative assessment tools, without undue burden on you. For instance, you might:

- provide practice multiple-choice questions corresponding to each of your identified course objectives, with answers and explanations;

- with practice essays and exercises, provide a self-assessment checklist or rubric for students to determine their level of performance;

- provide opportunity for students to join with peers to compare and revise their writings;

- provide practice short-essay questions corresponding to final course objectives, with model answers for student self-assessment;

- designate relevant computer-aided legal instruction lessons offered by commercial service providers, that include immediate feedback on selected answers;

- design online quizzes with automatic responses to student answers;

- offer to read and comment on practice answers to former exams; and

- provide handout exercises on subsidiary skills with answers.

Notice that of the above methods, only one requires the professor to examine individual student answers to provide constructive critique. The rest give the student feedback without direct professor involvement as to any individual answer. Self-assessment is a skill useful in professional practice. Lawyers make constant adjustments in their professional performances from a range of contextual feedback mechanisms. Professors may resist designing interim formative assessments, believing that they will require substantial additional professor time in individual assessment. That belief is mistaken. You have many ways to provide feedback without adding to professor time, once you choose, design, and implement the method.

On the other hand, individual assessment of at least some students on some measures has at least two advantages. First, it gives you feedback on your own instruction. Formative assessments like computer-aided instruction can give you automatic feedback on student performance. When you individually read and score student formative assessments, you can evaluate directly how students are performing under your instruction. Second, it gives students additional confidence in your commitment to them and their instruction. They benefit from your individual critique. Use formative assessment as guide, challenge, inspiration, and tool, for both yourself and your students.

Learning. To appreciate how formative assessment can aid student learning, first recall Bloom's Taxonomy of Educational Objectives. Learning includes not only knowledge, at the base of the pyramid, but also, in successively higher levels, comprehension, application, analysis, synthesis, and evaluation. The first two levels, knowledge and comprehension, are substance oriented, meaning that formative assessment should focus on key terms, principles, and concepts comprising the course content. Summative assessment should generally not focus on these subsidiary levels of learning. Clients seldom retain lawyers to provide definitions. They instead seek higher-level skills. Testing subsidiary skills can provide both you and your students with a formative guide to student levels of learning. You can diagnose, adjust, and remediate lower-level learning, or confirm, encourage, and move on to higher-order learning, with early and consistent formative assessment of subsidiary skills learning.

Designing assessments of subsidiary knowledge is not difficult. For example, in a first-year course, an instructional objective at the knowledge level might require the student to list various categories of tort or crime, identify correct statements of policy and rationale, and perhaps identify applicable codes and leading case names. A question like, "What is the standard of review on appeal from an administrative agency?" or request like, "Name the two main policies widely cited to support tort law," are tests of subsidiary knowledge. By contrast, questions like "What is your evaluation of whether plaintiff will prevail?" and "What additional information would you need to determine whether plaintiff has a claim?" test higher-order reasoning. Notice that the verbs used to elicit higher-order performances change, from simpler tasks like to *name* and *list*, up to more complex performances like to *evaluate* and *weigh*. An appendix lists the progressively higher levels of Bloom's Taxonomy of Educational Objectives together with verb cues for each level of objective. Good instructional design builds through progressively higher levels of reasoning.

If students meet the requirements on subsidiary skills assessment, then you can move forward satisfied that students need no further instruction on those knowledge components. Poor results should lead you to offer additional resources and reviews, and revise your instructional methods regarding those items. Individual students who meet or exceed the subsidiary skills requirements may want to supplement their studies with other developmental co- and extra-curricular activities. Individual students who fail to meet the requirements should seek outside academic support, curtail extra-curricular activities, obtain testing for accommodation, change study habits or partners, or increase study time and effort.

The four levels of higher learning (application, analysis, synthesis, and evaluation) involve methods more than substance. They accordingly require a different form of assessment. For example, application of law knowledge begins with identifying issues, what law professors commonly know as *issue spotting*. Issues are legitimate points of controversy that may affect the outcome. Formative assessment should help students recognize issues. Spotting issues can involve identifying key events out of a series of events, matching events to legal theories, or determining what aspect of the theory (for instance, which element of a claim or charge) is in genuine dispute.

Formative assessment can and should sharpen each of these application skills. You can draft multiple-choice or short-essay questions, for instance, challenging students to identify significant events as in, "Which of the above facts best supports the plaintiff's battery claim?" or "At what point did the facts first support a burglary charge?" You can also draft questions testing applicable theories as in, "What charge do the above facts support?" or "What defense would the defendant most likely assert?" You can also draft questions testing disputed elements as in, "Which element should the defendant's motion to dismiss argue?" or "Which element of the charge is missing?" Assessment can cover all these application skills. You can separately draft test items to assess student skills at analysis, synthesis, and evaluation levels. Testing all higher levels of learning, once students have acquired the subsidiary knowledge and comprehension, gives students both formative practice and helpful feedback.

Summative Assessment. Law professors should also determine whether students meet minimum criteria to pass the course. Already, you should see how important to summative assessment it is for you to have defined instructional objectives in a clear and systematic manner.

When you do not define objectives, you risk passing and failing students competitively based on how they perform in contrast to one another (the dreaded curve) rather than against a defined performance standard (learning objectives). Depending on the class's overall performance, you will inevitably either condemn some students to fail even when they could have met or did meet a reasonable performance standard, or you will permit some students to pass when they in fact did not meet the minimum performance standard and may have succeeded only in non-critical preliminary steps to the required performance. Professors should generally not design education with the intent of failing a certain percentage of students.

Do not make the test more difficult than the anticipated conditions of practice simply to norm-reference and fail a certain percentage of students. If the skill and conditions are easy, then the test should be easy, and if hard, then hard. Norm-referenced grading detracts from an academic environment. Students understandably compete under norm-referenced grading, rather than cooperate and collaborate. Some of the worst competitive practices one hears about in law school and other academic environments, such as hiding reference materials or tearing out key pages of a print resource, one can readily link to norm-referenced grading. Criterion-referenced grading can restore an academic environment, fostering study groups, collaboration on projects, and other healthy student peer support and interaction.

Drafting. Different schools of thought and different practices exist on when to draft your final assessment. Many if not most professors write their final examinations for the school's administrative deadline near the end of the term. Yet one can make good arguments for writing the final summative assessment much earlier, immediately after you write the course objectives and before you design instruction. Doing so ensures that your summative assessment aligns with course objectives rather than choosing something subsidiary that you found especially interesting during the course of instruction. Do not diagnostically test subsidiary concepts on final summative examination. Final exam is too late for diagnosis. Final exams are time for performance. You should design your final exam with the intent to test whether students meet defined course objectives. Writing the final examination early focuses your instruction around the course objectives you designed. Secretaries who must prepare, administrators who must review, and students who must take your examination will appreciate and respect your instructional integrity.

Validity. Invalid exams are a common problem in law schools where professors often have little or no training in exam preparation and almost surely none in psychometrics. To accomplish assessment's purposes, examinations must be valid, reliable, and fair. A valid exam is one that measures student competence on the instructional objectives, meaning an exam that measures what the professor intends it to measure. The Law School Admissions Test (LSAT) intends to measure probable law school success. It seeks predictive validity. By contrast, law school examinations intend to measure competence in course objectives. Law school examinations seek content validity. Exam-preparation errors tend to arise around poor specification of the exam task (unknown objectives combined with imprecise calls of the question), interdependence of tested materials (miss one part, miss all), and presupposing knowledge not taught. Law professors who fail to define learning objectives tend to write less valid exams. For example, if you assess writing skills in a course in which you taught doctrine but not writing, then your test will be invalid. If you test procedural knowledge when you taught doctrinal knowledge for which procedure was not a prerequisite, then your test will be invalid. Instruct and test on specific objectives.

Relatedly, using a broad call of the question invites students to misinterpret your intent. Students perform exactly as you requested but not to your instructional objective. If you must use a broad call ("Who wins?"), then consider combining it with a narrow follow-up call that ensures appropriate detail and focus ("Also, identify and discuss the claim and its elements justifying your conclusion."). Consider another example, this one of several interdependent test items. You might have designed a series of successive questions based on a single scenario, in which the answer to the first question determines the answers to the rest of the questions:

1. Which is the best claim?

    a. State the evidence you would present to support the claim.

    b.   Analyze the elements of the claim.

    c.   Cite the code section in support of the claim.

    d.   Identify any administrative filings the claim requires.

Notice that an otherwise capable student who answered the first question wrong may get all other questions wrong, too, because of the initial error. The first issue, "Which is the best claim?" may even have implicated a judgment call with some discretion to choose alternative answers. Yet the otherwise capable student would have lost all other points available on the question because of the interdependence of test items. Avoid these invalidity errors. One of the most disappointing instructor tasks is to have to fail a student whose other work indicates obvious capability, and perhaps even excellence, when the student made an initial error on interdependent test items that cost the student more points than passing could afford. Write independent test items as far as you are able.

Reliability. Assessment should also be reliable. A reliable test is one that produces a score unaffected by chance, error, or grader inconsistency, meaning one that would produce consistent results for any one student across more than one examination on the same objectives. Two examples of unreliability that may be relatively common in law school assessment are (1) unrepresentative content sampling and (2) scoring inconsistency. An exam has content reliability only if it tests a broad enough sample of course content. Multiple-choice and short-answer test items can broaden sampling and increase content reliability if those test items align to learning objectives. Consider constructing exams against a checklist of learning objectives, with the subjects each identified as high, medium, and low priority. Doing so will enable you to confirm that you have drawn a representative sampling. Future employers of your school's graduates would probably prefer that you have tested graduates on all or most high-priority objectives, many medium-priority objectives, and fewer low-priority objectives, to ensure graduates' capability to perform core competencies. Reviewing past exams in this manner will assist you to determine and adjust the proper distribution and priority of tested items.

Fairness. Assessment should also be fair, meaning conducted under circumstances most likely to measure genuine student capability without undue environmental and attitude effects. For instance, imagine administering a summative assessment (one that counted substantially toward student final grades) without notice. Some students would perform to capability while others would not, depending on random effects of schedule, rest, review, and preparedness. To increase fairness, law professors should reveal test logistics, form, scope, and content early enough in instruction for students to prepare and thereby minimize random effects. Law school final examinations are always complex in their content but can also be complex in form, point and time allocations, and related structure. Reduce attitude effects and increase fairness by providing advance information in the course syllabus about the following:

- the relative weight of the final exam to mid-term and other assessments (for example, 20% mid-term, 80% final exam);

- the type of questions (multiple choice, short answer, essay, etc.);

- the number of questions of each type (20 multiple choice, 4 short answers, 2 long essays, etc.);

- their relative points weight (60 points for multiple choice, 120 points for essays, etc.);

- limitations on answer length (three sentences for short answer, two pages for short essays, etc.);

- open or closed book conditions;

- other permissible exam resources (outlines, indexes, flash cards); and

- permissible tools (rulers, calculators).

Disclosing information about exam content well before the exam can also reduce attitude effects and increase fairness. An exam notice early in the course can include book, chapter, and page citations, case and code citations, references to professor-generated lists of concepts, and other statements identifying exam content. Some professors indicate throughout the course the priority level of various concepts as high, medium, or low. All concepts may be fair game on the final examination, but prioritizing concepts for students and testing primarily higher-priority concepts can help students focus on, learn, and perform well on priority concepts. You can and probably should tell students what topics are most important. You can and probably should tell students other test detail like the significance of case titles, act names, and code section numbers to exam scoring. If you intend to score students higher for giving names of specific cases or citing specific code section numbers, then notice of that intent increases exam fairness. Students should know your scoring criteria because, presumably, you have aligned your criteria to learning objectives. You want students to perform to the best of their abilities. Stating criteria in advance can improve performance. Stating criteria is not giving students the answers. It is giving them a chance.

Forms. To choose a proper form of assessment (essay, fill-in-the-blank, multiple choice, matching, live performance, portfolio), first identify the type of objectives (intellectual, verbal, textual, attitudinal) you wish to test. Doing so is easy with well-written objectives that state performance terms ("list," "advise as to," "draft"). It is not easy when objectives state preliminary indicator behaviors ("recognize," "recall") and covert behaviors ("understand," "know"). Once you identify the performance terms, you can match the form of test item to the type of objective. For instance, you should not use a multiple-choice question to test an attitudinal objective requiring the display of positive professional identity in a discussion forum. An essay exam or live performance would be the preferred choice. Conversely, you need not test with an essay exam an objective that requires simple choosing or sorting best tested by multiple-choice or matching test items. For other examples, you would best test oral advocacy skill by live performance, drafting prowess by displaying representative work in a portfolio, doctrinal knowledge by multiple-choice question, and synthesis of policy rationales by essay question.

Conclusion. Just as matching the test items to the performance, as indicated by objective type, is important, matching test conditions to the conditions for the desired performance is also important. Matching test to professional-practice conditions helps ensure that students who pass the test will be able to perform under practice conditions. Item difficulty should also match the anticipated practice conditions. The following two chapters address again these and other drafting issues, on specific forms of assessment. Developing the measurement (scoring) instrument is a separate step from writing the test. A subsequent chapter addresses scoring rubrics and grading.

> ***Exercise 10***
> Based on what you learned in this chapter, create two formative assessments around key concepts in the subject matter you teach. Design the assessments in ways that provide constructive feedback to students, help students identify their level of performance, and you can readily manage.

Chapter 11

Multiple-Choice Questions

How to Make Them Meaningful

Introduction. To assess effectively using multiple-choice questions, first understand their preferred forms and uses. Two common forms of assessment for law school instruction are multiple-choice questions and essay questions. Law school assessment comes in many forms, from the multiple-choice and essay questions on first-year exams, to seminar papers, moot court briefs, and simulated skills performances, all the way to representation of clients in law school clinics. Yet multiple-choice questions remain common. This chapter helps you recognize their advantages and disadvantages, explore their proper design, and guide you in drafting reliable and valid questions of your own.

Advantages. Law school professors differ in their opinions on the value of multiple-choice questions. Multiple-choice questions have some obvious advantages. The objective form of multiple-choice questions eliminates unreliably subjective scoring. Automatic scoring also eliminates professor scoring time. Their individual brevity also allows a professor to use many of them at once, thus distributing assessment more widely than some other forms of assessment. Wide distribution of assessment increases validity (alignment to objectives).

A more-obvious reason for law professors to use multiple-choice questions is that they are a primary form of assessment for bar examination. The Multistate Bar Examination used in nearly every state is a multiple-choice examination, as is the Multistate Professional Responsibility Exam used in most states. One cannot pass a bar examination and obtain a law license without some facility as to multiple-choice questions. That reason alone warrants their use (although certainly not to the exclusion of other forms of assessment). If graduates faced no bar exam, then professors could assess through simulation of practice skills. Yet graduates who cannot pass the bar exam will never get to use those practice skills. Multiple-choice questions help the student prepare for what will be the graduate's ticket to practice.

Disadvantages. Some law school professors believe that for all their value, multiple-choice questions have their disadvantages. The major limitation to multiple-choice questions is that they permit only one motor performance—circling letters on a numbered sheet. If only law practice were so simple. A student could be brilliant at the cognitive skills required to answer multiple-choice questions, having outstanding proficiency at circling lettered answers, but have none of the grammatical, writing, oral, interpersonal, and other affective skills required of every lawyer. In that sense, relying solely or too heavily on multiple-choice questions for either formative or summative assessment can be disadvantageous to the broader goals of professional instruction.

While recognizing this one major limitation, do not underestimate the power of well-designed multiple-choice questions. A common misconception is that multiple-choice questions address only lower levels of learning. Once again, Bloom's Taxonomy of Educational Objectives describes learning as occurring at several levels, from recall (simple memorization) at the lowest level, to understanding (the ability to put a recalled concept in one's own words), through application, synthesis, and evaluation. Analysis has shown that multiple-choice questions can test learning at all these levels. Consider this multiple-choice question as an example:

\#. A vehicle struck a pedestrian at a stop intersection. Police investigated at the scene. An ambulance took the pedestrian to the hospital. The pedestrian, who was a job superintendent for a municipality, missed several weeks of work. The pedestrian filed a negligence action against the vehicle driver, claiming that the driver had failed to stop at the sign at the intersection. The driver's motor-vehicle insurer assigned a lawyer the defense of the case. Which of the following is the best discovery plan in the lawyer's defense of the case?

A. Depose the vehicle driver, FOIA request the driver's driving records, and subpoena the driver's medical and employment records.

B. Depose the pedestrian, FOIA request the police report, and subpoena the pedestrian's medical and employment records.

C. Depose the investigating police, FOIA request the pedestrian's driving records, and subpoena the municipality's job records.

D. Hire an expert for accident reconstruction, and request an independent medical examination of the pedestrian.

The above multiple-choice question tests all levels of Bloom's Taxonomy, from recall, understanding, and application of the elements of negligence, to synthesis of those elements and evaluation of discovery plans. (The correct answer, by the way, is choice B.) Notice, too, that the question tests both doctrinal knowledge and performance skills. Well-drafted multiple-choice questions can test not only every level of learning but also combinations of knowledge, ethics, and skills. Now consider some general drafting guidelines for well-designed multiple-choice questions.

Drafting Guide. A director of testing for the National Conference of Bar Examiners (the organization responsible for the Multistate Bar Examination and Multistate Professional Responsibility Exam) urged that you draft multiple-choice questions with the goal of preparing students for law practice. Fundamental points include:

- test the application of important legal principles, not the recall of minor concepts;
- help students respect law practice (rather than to see it as the formal resolution of artificial and unimportant disputes) by using fact patterns that students are likely to encounter in law practice (not trite and unrealistic events whose only purpose is to test a legal concept); and
- provide all necessary facts and other information, especially the applicable law if it varies from jurisdiction to jurisdiction. The question's fairness may require you to identify the rule's authority, source, or breadth, meaning for instance whether it is a majority or minority rule, common-law or code rule, federal or state rule, or rule of a specific jurisdiction.

To write valid multiple-choice questions (those that test priority knowledge), you must also know what you are teaching and testing—in other words, your course objectives. Following are steps in their best order for writing valid multiple-choice questions:

1. List the legal concepts you are teaching.

2. Label the concepts you are teaching as high, medium, and low priority.

3. Select a suitably wide distribution of concepts to test, meaning to choose from all parts of your list.

4. Examine your selections to ensure that you have distributed testing of high-, medium-, and low-priority concepts.

    a. Test all high-priority concepts.

    b. Test most medium-priority concepts.

    c. Test few low-priority concepts.

5. Draft a multiple-choice question for each concept you desire to test.

Notice that the above, systematic manner of choosing test items eliminates duplicate test items. It is important to avoid testing the same concept several times because doing so may exclude the testing of other important concepts while confounding results. Distribution of test items is also important. Testing all or nearly all high-priority concepts, most medium-priority concepts, and few low-priority concepts will produce an exam of appropriate difficulty (not overly hard or easy) and discrimination (rewarding better-prepared students). Also, limit to three or fewer the number of judgments the student must make to deduce the correct answer. Requiring students to make, retain, and accumulate several decisions on different issues all at once decreases the reliability of exams, when considering time, environment, and performance pressures. Together, these practices will increase the validity and reliability of the multiple-choice portion of your exam. Now consider some specific multiple-choice design guidelines.

The Stem. A multiple-choice question has three parts, the stem, the lead-in, and the options. The stem is the fact pattern that creates the context for the legal analysis expected of the student. In law school multiple-choice questions, the stem often includes not only the facts but also the procedural context. Consider the following example of a stem that includes both facts and procedural context:

> A woman resided in a home into which a plane crashed, destroying the home. The woman was not at home at the time of the plane crash and was not hurt. A reporter covering the plane crash obtained contact information for the woman's son and sent the son an erroneous message stating that the plane crash killed his mother. The son was severely distressed when he received the erroneous email message. The son later sued the reporter, whose lawyer moved to dismiss for lack of duty.

The first four sentences of the above stem state the facts. The procedural context is the last sentence, "The son later sued the reporter, whose lawyer moved to dismiss for lack of duty." The procedure necessary to pose the proper question often appears at the end of the stem. When you state the procedural context while systematically varying it from question to question, you test students' ability to use legal knowledge in its practice context.

Reflection

> - Consider making an orderly list of the procedural and practice contexts in which students will use their legal knowledge, sharing the list with students.
> - Design practice test items for each context, and instruct students so that they learn how to use their new legal knowledge in those contexts.
> - Then, and only then, use those procedural contexts in your summative multiple-choice questions. Doing so ensures the validity, reliability, and fairness of your multiple-choice questions.

For example, a torts professor could list the stages through which torts practitioners perform, from intake, through pleading, to discovery, pretrial motions, alternative dispute resolution, trial, post-trial proceedings, appeals, and conclusion of the representation. Each of those stages has multiple practice contexts from which the torts professor could draw procedural context for multiple-choice questions. The professor would share with students the list of stages, contexts, and associated possible question calls, to ensure that students know these practice contexts. Take as an example the pretrial-motion stage. Summary judgment may be one motion that a defendant would file pretrial. An associated question call might be, "How should the trial court rule on defendant's motion?" or "What evidence should plaintiff produce to defeat defendant's motion?" Sharing with students in advance of examination the possible question calls in their procedural context ensures that the exam is testing doctrinal knowledge without causing students to answer incorrectly for lack of procedural knowledge. Doing so also teaches them substantial procedural knowledge.

Here is a paraphrased list of other drafting guides advocated by the National Conference of Bar Examiners for the multiple-choice stem:

- The stem should contain all facts necessary to answer the question. Avoid using additional facts in the answer options.

- The stem's language should be plain English. Avoid legalese and terms likely to be unfamiliar to English-second-language students.

- Include in the stem only the minimum number of actors needed for the fact pattern to test the concept. Do not have additional actors in the stem whose presence is of no consequence to the analysis.

- Describe actors by functional definitions ("the client," "the contractor") and common nouns ("the mother," "the husband") rather than by proper names ("Mary," "Joe").

- Minimize quotes. Do not include facts designed to trick students. Students should readily understand the facts.

- Avoid events and descriptions that are salacious, sensational, political, or humorous. Especially avoid attributions that reflect gender, ideological, racial, religious, and other bias.

- Avoid adjectives. Favor actions. Think Hemingway, not Faulkner.

The Lead-In. The second part of a multiple-choice question after the stem is the lead-in. The lead-in is the short question that tells the student what performance the professor expects. According to the National Conference of Bar Examiners testing director, the key to the lead-in is that a student must be able to answer it without referring to the answer options. A lead-in that states simply, "Which of the following is correct?" does not describe for the student the expected performance. The lead-in should instead identify the performance as in, "Which of the following is the best evaluation of the claim?" or "Which of the following is the most likely decision on the motion?" The stem and lead-in should together provide enough information for the student to make the analysis called for by the lead-in, without reading the answer choices.

One reason for this independent design of stem and lead-in from the answer choices is that it better approximates law practice. In law practice, no one is giving the lawyer the answers from which to choose. Lawyers must work from given facts and issues to arrive at conclusions (strategies, evaluations, opinions, approaches). The multiple-choice lead-in should mimic the natural performances expected of lawyers. It may surprise you to consider that with the right lead-in, multiple-choice questions can test clinical, strategic, and evaluative skills, not just analytic prowess. Consider the four sets of lead-ins below, each testing different skills. Consider drafting for your own use, while also sharing with students, a guide to the lead-ins you will use on the multiple-choice questions for your course relating to its practice field:

I. Clinical Skills
Where would you most expect to find evidence supporting the claim?
What advice would you best offer the client?
How should the lawyer respond to opposing counsel?
What issue should the lawyer resolve before advising her client?
What information does the lawyer need to proceed?
What question should the lawyer ask next?

II. Analytic Skills
Given the above facts, which tort has the man committed?
What is the biggest obstacle to the farmer's relief?
What rule should the judge apply?
If the manufacturer prevails, then what will be the most likely reason?
What additional facts must the lawyer prove?
How should the court rule on the rancher's motion?

III. Strategic Skills
Whom should the worker sue for a recovery in tort?
Which source will be most helpful?
Which witness will be most helpful to the trespasser's claim?
Which of the following arguments would be most helpful?
To survive a summary-judgment motion, what evidence must the shopper present?

IV. Evaluative Skills
Should the owner collect damages?
Is the evidence probative of the woman's liability?
Who is most likely to prevail as between the host and guest?
What will be the probable outcome of the defense?
Which is the best defense to raise by motion?
Which of the following causes of action is most likely to be successful?

The Options. The options are the answer choices from which the student must choose, for the one answer most closely matching the conclusion the student has drawn from the stem and lead-in. Psychometricians call the correct answer the *key* and the incorrect answer choices the *distractors*. A National Conference of Bar Examiners testing director urged that the correct key answer must be *clearly better* than the distractor options. Consider each of the following additional National Conference of Bar Examiner recommendations when drafting your multiple-choice questions:

- The options should have parallel language and structure.

- The options should be short. Favor single words and short phrases.

- The options should not contain additional facts.

- The options should avoid conditions like "No unless…" and "Yes if…," if those conditions add facts.

- The options should avoid "All of the above," "None of the above," and "A and B but not C" options.

- Each question should be independent of every other. No referring to the prior question for facts.

Conclusion. The multiple-choice questions you have seen on law school examinations and recall from your bar examination may have looked different from the ones described above. Several years ago, the National Conference of Bar Examiners hired a director of testing trained in psychometrics (the branch of psychology having to do with standardized testing) who previously held the same position for the organization responsible for medical board examinations. The new director judged the old-style bar-exam multiple-choice questions to be insufficiently valid and reliable, and instituted the new form advocated above. Congratulations on completing this chapter on multiple-choice questions. Remember, practice (at drafting multiple-choice questions) makes perfect. Drafting sound questions is a more complex art than one might expect but a satisfying and purposeful one when done properly.

Exercise 11

Examine the last multiple-choice questions you gave or those you are currently planning to give. Assess each question to see if it conforms to the guidelines outlined in this section. Then re-draft the set to comply with those guidelines.

Chapter 12

Essay Questions

Writing to Match Course Objectives

Introduction. To assess effectively using essay questions, you should know how to write and score them to match your learning objectives. When you use essay questions, their design and scoring is important to achieving the goals of either formative assessment (to foster improvement) or summative assessment (for purposes of grading).

Use. Essay questions are good for some objectives but not for others. Think again of Bloom's Taxonomy of Educational Objectives. Other forms of assessment like multiple-choice, true/false, and fill-in-the-blank questions are better tests of lower-order knowledge (recall) and understanding (paraphrase). Although those other assessment forms can test higher-order application, evaluation, and synthesis, well-designed essay questions have the peculiar advantage of testing higher-order thinking while also requiring students to *exhibit in writing* all levels of learning. Essay questions combine relevant performance skills (lawyers write) with relevant reasoning.

For example, consider which of the following you would prefer to test with essay questions rather than multiple-choice, true/false, or fill-in-the-blank questions:

(i) the definition of premeditation to establish a murder charge;

(ii) the standard of review on appeal from an administrative decision;

(iii) the relative strengths of various tort claims in a vehicle accident; and

(iv) the reasons why a services contract is or is not enforceable.

The tort-claim and contract-enforcement matters ((iii) and (iv)) would make better items for essay questions because they require higher-order application, analysis, and evaluation. The crime-definition and review-standard issues ((i) and (ii)) would make better items for multiple-choice or fill-in-the-blank questions because they involve lower-order recall rather than higher-order application and evaluation. Choose essay questions for the right, higher-order uses.

Components. Myths aside, there is more to an effective essay question than a good fact pattern. An effective essay question has several components, some of them immediately evident to the student and some not. An effective essay question begins with a fact pattern of appropriate length and level of complexity, one that adequately supports the issue, analysis, evaluation, and synthesis that you mean to engender. It also includes an appropriate call of the question to elicit the right student performance. It also involves assigning a point allocation to the question. Drafting also includes a model answer and scoring rubric, components that students do not see when taking the test.

You may find it best to first outline the scoring rubric before drafting anything else. You may then find it best to draft the exam and model answer, while revising the scoring rubric, concurrently rather than consecutively. Writing a sentence or two of the question, and then an associated paragraph of the model answer, and then revising the scoring rubric for that section, before returning to write the next sentence or two of the question, can help you generate facts and answers tied to the scoring rubric, while linking components to one another. It also keeps you from forgetting what it was you were trying to test and score as you drafted that wonderful fact pattern. Finally, essay and other questions should include the point value so that students can properly allocate time among test items. Just *when* you draft each component is your choice, but appreciate how complex these various components, their relationship, and their criteria make the process of exam drafting. Do not leave the task for the last minute.

Planning. Drafting effective essay questions requires planning. Begin with establishing the course objectives you should test. This process may include determining what subject matter, priority level (low, medium, or high), and skill level (knowledge, understanding, application, evaluation, or synthesis) multiple-choice or other portions of the exam have already tested. As the chapter on assessment suggested, distributing test items across subject matter, priority level, and skill level makes for more valid and reliable testing. Once you have chosen the topics, priority levels, and skill levels to test, you can sketch out a scoring rubric based on those choices. Test items begin with discerning the objectives. When test items invent new objectives rather than assess predetermined objectives, you increase the probability of alignment problems. You may test what you did not teach.

Reflection
- Compare your last essay exam, model answer, and scoring rubric, to your course objectives.
- Did you test an appropriate distribution of those objectives? What opportunities do you have for making a more sensitive distribution that ensures that your next essay questions test all high-priority concepts, most medium-priority concepts, and fewer low-priority concepts?
- Periodic, systematic review of past examinations can help you generate additional appropriate test items, ensuring that examinations remain tied to course objectives, which you have aligned to bar examination and practice. Consider identifying two course objectives that you did not test but that you feel you should next time.

Fact Patterns. When drafting fact patterns, professors should give due attention to party and witness names. Where possible, use role descriptions ("the contractor," "the manufacturer," "the landowner," "the golfer") rather than proper names. Requiring students to associate names with actions adds an additional conceptual task (memorizing names and matching them with roles) that is not a part of the purpose for examination. If you use proper names, then make them short or capable of abbreviation. Be sure to distinguish them from one another. Avoid single letters for names ("A," "D"). To reduce errors (both yours in drafting and scoring, and students' in writing), consider using clue names like "Chemco" for a chemical company, "Drugco" for a drug maker, "Farmer" for a farmer, and "Driver" for a motor-vehicle driver. Identify names with roles. Avoid proper names that have no meaning. Consider making your final-examination essay questions like the essay questions on the bar examination taken by the greatest number of your students. (More on this suggestion below.) Also, make your final-examination essay questions like the practice essays that you provide to students.

As to fact-pattern substance, make it realistic. Use fact settings that are likely to arise in law practice. Avoid trite disputes the serious consideration of which tends to cheapen the educational experience and undermine the value of law practice. Examine the fact patterns for your last few essay questions. What was their source? Law professors draw fact patterns from cases they saw from the bench, their own former cases in law practice, other lawyers' cases in law practice, reported cases, events in the news, and Restatements or other treatises or commentary. They also make them out of whole cloth from their own imagination or assemble them from various combinations of the above. All these sources are appropriate, within the guidelines suggested above. Validity, reliability, and fairness are the touchstones. Fact patterns should elicit relevant legal knowledge, be sufficiently clear and concise as to measure the use of that knowledge rather than other memorization or reading skills, and be consistent with the expectations you established for the examination.

Question Calls. Take special care in drafting your call of the question. The call of the question is the statement at the end of the fact pattern that elicits student performance. The form of the call of the question determines what level of learning you are testing, whether, for instance, application with analysis, evaluation, or synthesis. Consider a call of the question to "identify, discuss, and evaluate each of the worker's tort claims for her personal injury, including defenses." The call of the question tests application, analysis, and evaluation. Students must recall and apply their law knowledge in a test of claim spotting ("identify"). They must also analyze claims, elements, and defenses ("discuss"). They must also weigh the relative merits of claims ("evaluate"). Other calls might limit students to analysis ("Discuss the merits of the prosecutor's charge.") or evaluation ("State the probability that the buyer will prevail in her claim for specific performance, justifying your answer.").

Avoid unintentionally limiting student performance to one skill when you intend to test others. For instance, if you ask students to "identify all claims," then students could legitimately list just the names of tenable claims, without providing any discussion, analysis, and evaluation, as you may have intended. "Identify and discuss" or "identify and evaluate" would have been clearer. If you ask, "Who should prevail on appeal?" then you may get just the name of the party rather than an explanation. If you ask, "What is the correct charge?" then you may get the name of the charge without an explanation of why it is correct. If you ask, "What is the main issue?" then you may get the issue and not an analysis of how a court should decide it. If you intend to limit consideration to one party or claim, then clearly state so as in, "Identify and discuss only the contractor's claims." Expressly limiting consideration to certain parties may be wise, especially with complex fact patterns involving multiple actors. Broad calls like "identify and discuss all claims" create risks that students will spend too much time on parties or claims you regard as subsidiary.

Model Answers. Essay questions make it harder to grade consistently. As indicated further in the following chapter on grading, subjectivity in grading is a major problem with essay questions. Drafting model answers before you submit the final exam can reduce scoring subjectivity. When you take your own test, you may see additional claims and issues that you did not intend to test, allowing you to eliminate the facts that gave rise to them, to ensure that students address only what you intend to assess. Do not subjectively decide later not to award points for legitimate student answers that were not what you intended to write (but did write) into the fact pattern. Model answers can also help students evaluate their exam performance on their own, which may be a significantly more meaningful process for their learning than simply receiving a letter grade. Many institutions require model answers for this and other reasons.

> *Reflection*
> - What is your law school's policy on model answers?
> - If given discretion to provide a model answer, would you do so?
> - Consider making model answers from prior exams available to students who are preparing for your next exam. Model answers can help students recognize your criteria, especially if you have not articulated those criteria elsewhere.

Scoring. While other forms of assessment can be hard to write but are easy to score, essay questions can be harder to score than to write. Drafting a scoring rubric as you draft the essay question and model answer can reduce scoring time and inconsistency, and increase validity and reliability. You should ordinarily score numerically to increase the sensitivity of scoring measures. Assign enough points to the exam to enable you to allocate points to all questions and issues. One-hundred points may be a reasonable number for the entire test, with from ten to twenty points per essay. Further suggestions on scoring essay exams appear in the following chapter on grading.

> *Reflection*
> - Obtain from colleagues three examples of scoring rubrics different from your own. What are their relative merits and demerits?
> - Why do your colleagues use them instead of something closer to your own? Consider discussing essay question scoring with colleagues.

Time. Another criterion for an effective essay question is its fit to the time allotted. Many professors feel that severe time pressure distorts law school essay testing from its intended bar-passage and practice-competency measures. Law practice may or may not entail furiously efficient writing under the kind of severe time pressure that some law school final exams impose. When lawyers can avoid it, which may well be most of the time, practice under exam-like time constraints may well be unethical and unwise to the extent that it invites incompetence and malpractice. The point is that imposing time constraints too severely almost certainly distorts assessment's basic purpose of being a fair measure of recall, analysis, and writing competencies. It also disadvantages some students against others, again on a criterion that may not be important to practice. As a result, some professors deliberately ensure that students have more than the time required to complete a responsible answer, to give students with slower processing skills equivalent prospects.

One way to find a happy medium on question length and complexity is to mimic bar essays. You may find them to be surprisingly short and direct, although you may also find some of the rules and concepts that they test to be narrow or peculiar (especially when practitioners write the exams from their own experience without psychometric training). Obtain from the bar exam that most of your school's graduates take, the most-recent released essay questions on your subject. Then consider each of the following questions. How many words long is it? How long was your last essay on a similar topic? What learning level did its call of the question test (knowledge, understanding, application, evaluation, or synthesis)? What learning level did the call of the question on your last essay test? How long did the bar examinees have to answer it? How long did your students have to answer your last essay? These measures are appropriate comparison points. Consider making your essay questions more like the bar's essay questions.

Variety. If you have been writing essay questions for some time, and they are all beginning to sound alike, then you may be stuck in an unnecessary rut. In law school, most essay questions test issue spotting and the application of legal rules and concepts, which seems an obvious enough form. Yet can also test student ability to evaluate a statute, opinion, or similar material from public policy and related standpoints. You can also test student ability to synthesize, re-organize, or otherwise creatively structure course content, although these forms may be better reserved for upper-level students. Consider balancing multiple essay questions between questions requiring deep thought and questions that test course content comprehensively. Avoid giving students choices of which out of several questions to answer. Some students will waste time deciding which question to answer and then underperform, regretting their choice. You will also then be comparing student performances on different objectives with potentially different priority and level, which may inject unreliability and unfairness in grading. What most-common activity do lawyers in your subject field do when writing some form of analysis that you have never asked your students to do in an essay question? Consider including that form in your next set of essay questions. If you do, then be sure to first identify the skill in your course objectives and to instruct students in it. Give no surprises.

Conclusion. Finally, consider helping students prepare for your final-exam essay questions with the strategic advice that you feel will be most helpful. You would not be simply teaching test-taking skills. Exam-taking strategies transfer to work strategies. Consider encouraging students to look quickly through the essay questions, reading the calls of the question, before reading fact patterns for detail. Urge them to allocate time, stick to time allocations, outline answers, and follow their outlines. Encourage them to write down valuable thoughts that they feel they may forget. When absolutely stuck, students might try free association (writing any sensible thought related to the question's call) to prompt further recall. Tell students that if they have extra time, then to reread their answer and insert additional thoughts. Tell them that if they are running out of time, then to write down the main points. Students may have heard this encouragement before, but the fact that you took the time to reinforce it, even briefly, may reassure them of your interest in and expectation of their effective performance, which itself can improve performance.

> *Exercise 12*
> Draft a final-exam essay question (or examine a previously written essay question) ensuring that it aligns with your learning objectives, reflects high-priority concepts, uses a fact pattern that is likely to arise in law practice, contains an appropriate question call, fits the allotted time, and can be fairly and reliably scored.

Chapter 13

Grading

Scoring Rubrics and Grade Ranges

Introduction. To teach responsibly, one should have a basic grasp of the principles and practices of grading. Programs of professional education use assessment for more than formative purposes. Assessment also needs to be summative. When professors properly design and implement assessment, students who do not have the qualifications to serve the public with the minimum competence required of members of the profession in good standing should not graduate. The task of assigning grade ranges to assessment scores involves teaching and administration. It is an important aspect of the law professor's role. This chapter again draws from Michael Josephson's two-volume work on law school assessment, articles by Professor Sophie Sparrow and Lynn Daggett, and other sources drawing on psychometrics research. Psychometrics involves the measurement of cognitive capability. Organizations and agencies test individuals for many different purposes and against various criteria. Recognize and respect the summative purposes of your law school course's testing and grading.

Reflection

> - Recall the many areas in which organizations and agencies have tested you. Can you list five? Ten?
> - What were the exams trying to accomplish?

Criteria. As indicated above in the chapter on assessment, grading can be criterion referenced, in which students are measured against defined learning objectives, or norm referenced, in which students are measured against one another. Norm-referenced grading (also known as the dreaded *curve*) guarantees the relative success of some students and failure of others whether students achieve the instructional objectives or not. Under norm-referenced assessment, the institution's mission would establish the success and failure rate. For instance, graduates may have a limited number of positions available in some form of public service or other employment such as a military flight school. Training for those positions would include norm-referenced assessment to rank candidates so that the institution or agency fills only the limited number of positions. Indeed, a limited number of seats may exist for programs of professional education like law school. The Law School Admissions Test (LSAT) is a norm-referenced test, assigning LSAT scores to students in comparison with one another, not against defined criteria. By contrast, law school graduates are not competing to fill a specifically limited number of positions. Although large law firms may hire limited numbers of lawyers, most lawyers practice as sole proprietors or in small firms. A democratic republic and complex economy depend on large numbers of responsible citizens well versed in nuances of the law. Although not all would agree, some law professors and administrators hold that law school summative assessment should be primarily criterion referenced, not norm referenced.

Scoring. The first step toward completing summative assessment is to score numerically each examination that you are grading. Graders use numeric scores to evaluate examinations more sensitively. Numeric scoring of exams should be consistent with your scoring rubric, model answer, instructional alignment, and course objectives. Small scoring variations can have a significant impact on grades. Given the large number of students receiving grades term to term, inevitably a small number of points on a small number of examinations will eventually determine some unfortunate student's dismissal. Precise test instruments and systematic grading are critical. Psychometric studies find unreliability in scoring essay responses. Professor Josephson reported that a psychometrician found that lawyers whom the California Board of Bar Examiners trained to grade a single bar-exam question disagreed on pass/fail decisions one third of the time. In blind reviews, the *same grader* re-grading the *same essay* disagreed with the grader's own pass/fail decision 25% of the time, meaning that there was a one in four chance that passing or failing was random.

> *Reflection*
> - Have you ever taken an examination, the results of which surprised you sufficiently that you were tempted to investigate or did investigate the grading?
> - What evidence of grading accountability did you find, or would you have hoped to find, if you had investigated? Your students may find themselves in the same position with respect to your grading. Be prepared to support their inquiry to the extent that your institution allows or requires it. Prepare every summative examination as if students' opportunity to practice law depends on it and in a way that you can justify scoring and grading to them. Your institution may or may not require it, but responsible instruction does require it.

Rubrics. To reduce scoring error, draft written model answers and scoring rubrics with point allocations before student testing and scoring. Developing a scoring rubric as you grade may result in changes in your scoring practice from exam to exam. It also may result in scoring against measures other than those related to your course objectives and instruction. Draft the rubric first. Some educators will provide modified rubrics to students in advance of examination, to ensure that students understand expected performances. After you draft a rubric matching your course objectives, instruction, and exam, complete the written scoring rubric as you grade each exam so that you can attach a copy of it to the graded exam. Rubrics can save you substantial time spent scoring, in addition to ensuring exam validity. The design of the scoring rubric is up to you, but keep in mind that scoring rubrics may include point allocations for all forms of instructional objectives. For instance, you may allocate points to identifying claims and analyzing elements and defenses, as follows:

Plaintiff 1 v Defendant 1/negligence   ____/2
    Duty/standard of care   ____/2
    Breach/violation of statute   ____/2
    Cause-in-fact/substantial factor   ____/2
    Proximate cause/foreseeability   ____/2
    Damages/injury and distress   ____/2

You may also allocate points to other performances if you identified them as course objectives and provided the requisite instruction. For instance, you may allocate general points to the deductive order of analysis, inductive recognition of factual details and patterns, abductive estimation of issues for investigation, skill of evaluation, and ethics of investment and commitment:

General
    Deductive/logic/order   ____/3
    Inductive/patterns/detail   ____/3
    Abductive/investigation   ____/3
    Evaluation/judgment   ____/3
    Ethics/identity/investment   ____/3

To increase scoring consistency, consider scoring each item completely before scoring the next item, scoring all items of one kind without interruption, and re-scoring the first several exams you scored. These practices can reduce scoring anomalies due to distraction, gradual changes in scoring practices, and other variables. Total the points at the bottom of the rubric, including any additions for separately (machine-) graded multiple-choice questions. Detailed rubrics not only increase the objectivity of your grading but also reassure students and administrators of the accountability of your work and create evidence of student successes.

Students may find formative benefits to summative assessment, if you write helpful evaluations and comments on the exam or rubric, if the law school permits students to examine them after you complete grading. If you do write comments, then prefer those that alert students to their having met or departed from specific criteria, such as "This exam answer fails to identify the parties and claims as the call of the question required." Avoid using adjectives and other evaluations that have no verifiable measure, like "This exam answer is too long and too vague for credit." Also, avoid comparisons with other student performances that the criticized or lauded student cannot verify, like "This is the worst exam answer I have seen in years." Non-verifiable comparisons do not give students criteria against which to measure their own performance and the quality of your assessment and scoring, and may result in disrespect and resentment.

Grades. Once scoring is complete, you can assign letter grades based on scores. Assigning letter grades depends on criteria established by the law school's grade definitions. Law school graduates must pass the bar exam to practice law. That restriction makes bar-passage capability a principal criterion for law school summative assessment. Your law school's grade definitions should require you to determine as a threshold matter whether students can pass the bar because to advance a student who is not capable of passing the bar could mislead the student. How are law professors who have never written a bar exam, probably took a bar exam only once, and may have done so only many years ago still able to judge student capability at passing the bar? Law professors who have practice experience, read and write for practice journals, and continue to interact substantively with members of the practicing bar have constant reminders of the minimum knowledge possessed by members of the practicing bar, each of whom (after all) has passed the bar. Lawyers constantly draw on their sense of the law knowledge of other practitioners (including judges) when speaking and writing about the law. Some practitioners have outstanding law knowledge. Interaction with other practitioners will suggest less knowledge. You should draw on that sense of the law knowledge of less capable but still minimally qualified members of the bar when establishing your minimum requirements for passing your course. Unless your institution's grade definitions require that you do so, do not require students to demonstrate a level of excellence exceeding that which law practice requires.

You should also be able to articulate the difference between the extensive law knowledge of a practitioner in your course's field, and the more limited knowledge of a licensed lawyer who does not practice in your course's field. Think for a moment of two core concepts in your course that licensed lawyers who are not practicing in your course's field should still know and then two concepts that you would expect only a practitioner within your course's field to know. An example might be that lawyers who do not practice tort law should nevertheless know that (1) negligence claims require proof of duty, breach, causation, and damages, and (2) breach is a departure from the standard of care. Lawyers who practice tort law would also know that (1) violation of a safety statute is likely to be evidence of breach and (2) negligence law treats violation of a safety statute as negligence per se or as giving rise to a presumption or inference of negligence, depending on the jurisdiction. Your ability to match scores to grade ranges depends on making these kinds of nuanced judgments.

Grade Ranges. Recall the purpose of summative assessment and its principal bar-passage criterion. Depending on how your law school defines its grade ranges, the lowest "C" grade for your course should represent the performance of a lawyer who does not practice in your course's field but is still minimally capable of passing the bar. Think of lawyers who, although licensed, did not practice in your field, and with whom you communicated about your field (an occurrence that happens often, when you think about it). You have a sense of the limits of their knowledge of your field, which would include its rudiments. They passed the bar, and so for you to award a student a "C" for demonstrating similar knowledge may be appropriate, again depending on your law school's grade definitions.

Bar passage is not the only goal for law students, who are also preparing to practice law. Their practice goal makes practice capability a second principal criterion for law school summative assessment. Depending on how your law school defines its grade ranges, the lowest "A" grade for your course should match the performance of a lawyer who practices in your course's field. Again, although some variation would exist in the level of that knowledge from practitioner to practitioner, you know that level of knowledge from your interaction with practitioners in your field including your reading of and writing for practice journals. For you to award an "A" to students demonstrating similar knowledge may be appropriate, again depending on your law school's grade definitions.

Calculating Ranges. Once you have the above two points established (lowest "C" and lowest "A"), calculating preliminary grade ranges requires only simple mathematics. Assume a grade scale that includes letter grades A, A-, B, B-, C, C-, D, and F. Each letter grade will have a point range from the lowest score a student could receive and still earn that grade to the highest score for that grade, for instance, 93 to 100 for an "A." Once you have the determined the lowest "A" and the lowest "C" scores, you need only divide the total number of points between those two scores by the number of intermediate grade ranges that you need to establish (in the given grade scale, four) to get the size of the grade ranges. For instance, if your lowest "A" was a 93 and lowest "C" a 69, you have 24 points (93 minus 69) within which to establish 4 grade ranges, which is 6 points (24 divided by 4) per grade range. Your grade ranges of 6 points each would be "A" 93 to 100, "A-" 87 to 92, "B" 82 to 91, "B-" 76 to 81, and "C" 69 to 75. Given normal distributions, the lowest grade range "F" and the highest grade range "A" should ordinarily be significantly wider than the intermediate grade ranges, because some students will do much better or much more poorly than others, and their outlier performance should not distort the grade scale. That reason makes it even more appropriate to adopt the lowest "A" and lowest "C" scores to calculate grade ranges. On a scale of 1 to 100, for instance, an "F" might be 0 to 59 while an "A" might be 93 to 100.

Grade ranges need not be perfectly uniform but should be reasonably so. Knowledge accrues along a continuum. Setting aside the top grade range for "A" and the bottom grade range for "F," your law school's intermediate grade definitions were probably not written to produce a narrow range for one grade definition and significantly wider range for another. Students may see widely varying grade ranges as arbitrary or, worse, an intentional effort to keep them from getting a certain higher grade just outside of their own grade range. Note each of the following examples of clearly acceptable, clearly unacceptable, and probably acceptable grade ranges (especially if the distribution of individual grades justifies their pattern):

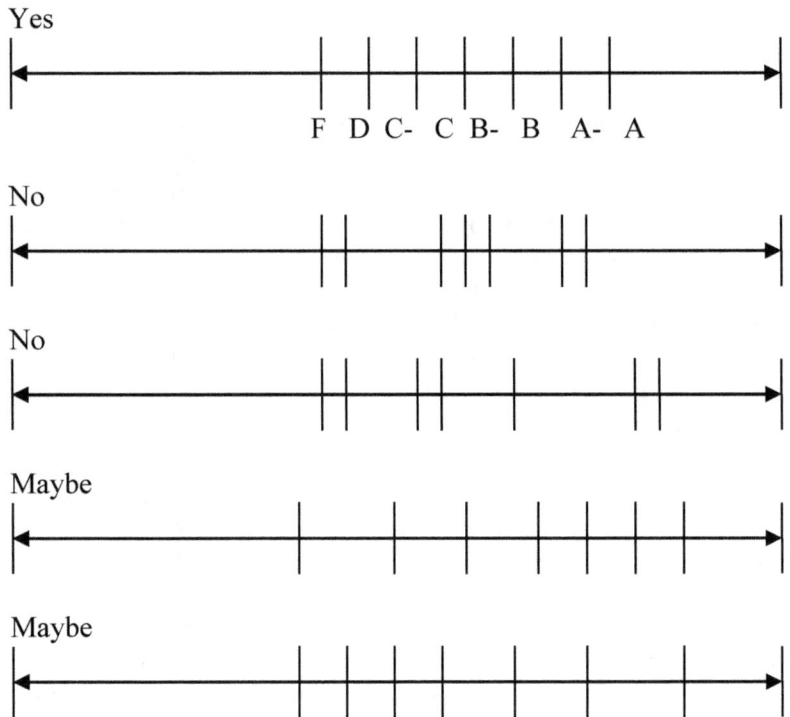

Normalizing. Determining your scores, grade ranges, and grades does not quite complete the process. In education, at all levels including professional schools, administrators have a role in ensuring that grades meet institutional definitions and standards. For instance, it is not unheard of for a just-terminated professor grading a last course to fail vindictively all or most students, obviously requiring administrative intervention. Even beyond those aberrations, many institutions norm grades among professors to reduce student angst, professor shopping, and disagreement among professors over "hard" and "soft" grading. A common means to norm grades is for departments to recognize historical ranges for overall class averages, say, from a 2.75 to 3.25, and to review grades with professors only when an overall class average falls outside of that range. Keep in mind that you have a responsibility not only to students but also to colleagues and institution over grading.

> *Reflection*
> - Are you an "easy" or "hard" grader?
> - What do students think of your grading practices relative to your colleagues' practices?
> - Do you know who the easy graders and hard graders are?
> - Do you think students know?
> - How does that knowledge affect relationships with your colleagues over grading practices?

Institutions also make intensive and helpful studies of enrollment profiles and attrition rates. These studies can help you adjust your grading practices. For instance, if entering student academic profiles improve due to more successful recruiting, but faculty members persist with traditional grade norms instead of adjusting them to improving student profiles, then faculty members may unintentionally fail a disproportionate percentage of capable students. For these and other reasons, those who have studied the subject tend to hold that professors should prefer limited institutional grade normalizing over no normalizing, if any normalizing is sensitive to enrollment screening, academic support, class size, and other program variations that may be good cause to support grade variation from class to class. Sharing grade information among professors can also help. Some professors grade high while others grade low. Some bunch grades in the middle while others distribute them widely or gather them around other points along the grade scale. Professors who see how differently they grade and how disparate are the patterns of grading tend to be more receptive to normalizing. Normalizing does not change a professor's ranking of students within a class.

Conclusion. Their significance to student advancement and achievement make scoring and grading daunting responsibilities. You can rest assured that you have met that responsibility by considering all and adopting some of the above practices. You can also explore the subject more deeply through other psychometrics resources. Summative assessment is a critically important subject. Consider it carefully, and respect it.

Exercise 13
Consider the grading practices outlined in this chapter. List the practices you would consider implementing for grading in your next teaching assignment.

Chapter 14

Vision

Experiences and Outcomes

Introduction. To teach most effectively, one should develop a deeper sense of the discipline of teaching and the fulfilling imperative of learning. The vision thing challenges many of us. Yet challenge is no reason to avoid, and instead good reason to embrace, a deeper teaching philosophy or vision. Students appreciate teaching skills. They also notice and appreciate teaching vision. They benefit from teaching craft but flourish under teaching spirit. Although vision tends to be personal (especially in the way that popular psychology and culture tend to define vision), this chapter suggests some approaches that may help. Consider connecting your vision to your institution and the community of teachers and learners whom you admire and wish to support.

> *Reflection*
> - What have you done to articulate a teaching vision for yourself and to share with students?
> - What prompted your efforts?
> - With whom did you share vision, and how (orally, in writing)?

> - Can you articulate a teaching vison now or at any other ready moment when asked?
> - Consider exploring and defining your teaching vision. You may be surprised by what doing so produces.

Personality. Many of the better-known inspirational writings on teaching center on the professor more than on students. Such valuable writings as Parker Palmer's *Courage to Teach* and his earlier and more overtly spiritual *To Know as We Are Known* promote intense self-reflection. They view teaching through an experiential lens, emphasizing the emotional, constructed, imaginative, and personal nature of the teaching experience and teaching identity. In their normative forms, they advocate teaching attributes like authenticity and actions like consistent disclosure of genuine self within a community valuing relationship and perspective—perhaps difficult to identify and achieve but possibly valuable even for that reason. The writings hope to help professors to fashion a dialogical self, leading to consciousness of the effect of one's presence on others, especially students. At times intensely constructivist, the writings seek self-knowledge through metaphor, fantasy, emotion, and extra-rationality (one supposes, what we used to call irrationality). In this mystical mix, the writings hope to lead professors to love of teaching and learning. So (tongue in cheek), right now in your teaching, are you Sisyphus, Cyclops, Jungle Boy, Spiderman, Rambo, Superman, or Iron Man, or do you care to choose another?

All parody aside, teaching has an intensely personal aspect. Professors have something to gain by attending to and even studying the personal experience of teaching. One way to do so, without making the teaching experience an unhealthily narcissistic endeavor, is to maintain an electronic teaching portfolio. Include within your teaching portfolio folders for reflection on teaching, service, and scholarship vision. Capturing from time to time a little inspiration on teaching is neither foolish nor dangerous and can instead be encouraging. Each time you read, hear, see, or think of something that sparks a teaching vision, make a note in the appropriate file in your vision folder. You might be surprised at the accumulation of insight and wisdom that can occur over time. Periodically review, reorganize, and refine those visions, and you may end up with sensitive and comprehensive statements of your teaching beliefs and faith. Looking back, you may also be surprised at how emotionally and spiritually rich the teaching experience is.

Portfolio. Then, to build on your teaching vision, create in your electronic portfolio a natural order and feedback loop. After creating your portfolio and its vision subfolder, create other subfolders at the same level for objectives, planning, and assessment. Notice the order: vision feeds objectives that guide planning that assessment evaluates and informs. Use these folders and subfolders constantly. Place every document that you create in one of these folders. Your resume or curriculum vitae, for instance, belongs in the assessment folder because it documents and supports evaluation of what you do. Your job description may belong in the objectives folders because it establishes the expectations for your role. In your planning folder, create subfolders for each course you teach. In each course's folder, create the same feedback loop of subfolders from vision to objectives, planning, and assessment. Then, for each course, put any inspiration for that course in the vision folder, your syllabi in the objectives folder, your slideshows and outlines in the planning folder, and your exams and scoring rubrics, and any course surveys you administer, in the assessment folder. Build these feedback loops into your everyday, working portfolio, and you will have organized your working life into a naturally and constantly reflective order. You will not only gain structure for your seemingly endless and chaotic activity, but that structure will constantly encourage your reflection over and improvement of that activity.

Outcomes. Thankfully, though, teaching is not all about us. Another and in some ways healthier approach to thinking gainfully about teaching vision is to consider teaching's most important outcomes, meaning the students whom you influence and graduates whom your faculty certifies as bar fit. Your teaching portfolio can gather evidence of student work, not merely your work. Law school accreditation standards require law schools to demonstrate appropriate learning outcomes. The Uniform Task-Based Management System created by the American Bar Association, Association of Corporate Counsel, corporate clients, and law firms, creates greater lawyer and law firm accountability in the efficient delivery of legal services. Law schools are equally accountable to produce graduates who have the practical business and management skills to understand client needs in the delivery of legal services.

Graduates, and the knowledge, skills, and ethics they possess, are law schools' central outcomes. Teaching vision should look to them more so than to us, the ones who teach them. A law professor's vision for graduates should be larger and more ambitious, inspired, detailed, and magnanimous than for the .

> *Reflection*
> - Whether you can articulate a vision for your teaching or not, can you articulate a vision for your students and their learning?
> - What would be that vision's principal features?
> - What would be its most appropriate sources (where would you look for student vision)?
> - Picture a student of yours now, as a graduate of your school later. What should that student's defining professional attributes be?
> - With what imagination and inspiration could you influence that student now?

With appropriate vision, research, and effort, we can answer these questions with some specifics. For example, Gerald Susskind has been studying and writing about the changes in global law practice for the past three decades. He recently posited these five kinds of lawyers who would survive and prosper through accelerating changes in law practice:

1. expert trusted advisers who speak new, novel, complex, high-value business solutions to their clients;

2. enhanced practitioner who will convey standardized legal products to clients at reduced costs without substantial personal interaction;

3. talented legal knowledge engineers who will develop standard documents and procedures for organization;

4. legal risk managers who will develop methods and systems to help clients control legal risks; and

5. legal hybrids who work in a multi-disciplinary fashion steeped in their client's business.

> *Reflection*
> - As you advise individual students, consider which of the above five kinds of lawyers you think their interests, talents, and callings best fit.
> - What have you done or can you do today to help these students along the educational and pre-career pathways to their best fit within the profession? Through efforts like these, you can make vision a practical tool in teaching and advising students.

Successes. Here is another example of a teaching vision that would be accountable to your law school's mission. To help your institution document its most important and successful outcomes, try writing a short biographical sketch of the law school experience and post-graduate placement and success of a recent graduate of your law school whom you feel that you influenced and whom you know is achieving a fulfilling measure of professional success. In your description, use at least once each of the following words or similar words that align with your institution's mission: affordable, career, challenge, community, competence, discipline, diverse, enjoy, explore, family, flexible, identity, master, mission, opportunity, prepared, professional, quality, ready, responsible, rigorous, second career, sensible, service, skill, social justice, success, support, tailored, and vision. Then make an electronic folder for that portrait, add other, similar graduate portraits from time to time, and with the graduates' permission share them with school administrators as the best evidence of your teaching and the institution's success. You can center your vision on the success of others in the way that teaching implies. You can also make it real, practical, personal, and authentic.

Significant Learning. What you might find by centering your teaching vision on the graduates whom you have influenced is that the learning outcomes you desire are much deeper, richer, and more complex than you previously imagined. Among the rich educational literature on higher and adult education is a recent book by Dee Fink titled *Creating Significant Learning Experiences—An Integrated Approach to Designing College Courses*. It suggests a new form of Bloom's Taxonomy of Educational Objectives, which has learning accumulating in six hierarchical steps from knowledge to comprehension, application, analysis, synthesis, and evaluation. The new form, labeled *taxonomy of* *significant learning*, characterizes learning as occurring in six simultaneous (rather than hierarchical) sectors. Those sectors include Bloom's knowledge and application, in one sector. They also include integration of professional knowledge, a human dimension to professional service, caring as a core purpose, and learning how to learn. Learning still depends first on acquiring an information fund that one can skillfully apply. Yet the new taxonomy also sees as significant, learning to learn, so that students can continually integrate new action logic into an expanding realm of practice. Learning skill also helps students learn about themselves and others, helping them commit to caring service. The graduates we most admire may be those who have become master learners, continually renewing a knowledge base to serve others in responsible and caring fashion. Masterful professional practice and successful personal life require mastery of learning. You need not confine your teaching vision to discipline mastery. It can include learning and other-discipline masteries.

Exploration. The above discussion shows that the educational literature is one way that you can expand your teaching vision. You can also deepen and enrich the learning environments you create and your own experience of them with disciplined exploration of fields related to education. Legal education can be practical without being anti-intellectual. Rigorous examination by others of some of our underlying assumptions can improve our own understanding to the point that we may be able to reach, serve, and inspire more students toward their own deep learning. A few examples follow, drawn from what committed intellectual explorers already know is an inexhaustible supply of rich resources. Deliberate thought and small actions over time can help accumulate teaching wisdom.

Reflection
- As you read these explorations, think of the last book you read expressly for teaching inspiration. How long ago did you read it?
- What is the next book you plan on reading for teaching inspiration?
- Do you track your teaching reading to ensure broad coverage and progressive development?
- Do you plan it?

> - How does teaching-reading come to your attention (through what list-serves, library liaisons, colleagues, staff members, mailings, meetings, and other sources)?

Thinking. Studies suggest that how students think of thought influences their learning. Epistemological beliefs (beliefs about thinking) influence how students approach and acquire new thought. Students can hold naïve or sophisticated beliefs about the certainty of knowledge, its structure, its sources, their ability to control its acquisition, and the speed of their acquisition. Students organize those epistemological beliefs into systems, some of which are effective for learning law and others of which impede learning. Epistemological beliefs affect learning both directly (causing students to accept or reject specific knowledge) and indirectly (influencing study habits). Law professors can influence students' epistemological systems by, for instance, encouraging students to attribute performance to controllable causes. You can teach students new epistemological beliefs that can make their learning more effective.

Epistemological beliefs have more to do with law practice than simply how law students acquire new law knowledge. Lawyers, too, depend on special ways of thinking about thinking, indeed on special forms of thought as action. How can law students learn more about lawyer thinking? Tradition, for an example important to lawyers, contains things that lawyers have not yet thought but that call for lawyers to bring into representation and action. Traditions of law practice may have something broader, deeper, and richer to share, if you prepare to hear and represent those thoughts about it. Traditional thought about what being a lawyer means is not simply a representation from the past but can also be something drawing the profession into the future. The traditions and experiences of law practice are so enormously rich that the untapped thoughts they contain for the future are also rich. To retain citizen trust and confidence, lawyers must transport an enormously complex and sophisticated justice system into the future in continuity with the rich traditions of the past. To do so, lawyers and law professors should think more deeply not only about law practice in the past but also about thinking, meaning one's study of thought. Epistemology is certainly an inter-disciplinary field that could influence your teaching vision.

> *Reflection*
> - Have you ever thought rigorously about what lawyers think about thought?

Truth. Lawyers are also obviously concerned with truth. How can law students understand truth more deeply? One can and should associate truth with being. Thinking is responding to a call that the subjects of thought bring forth from their essence. Truth is not (as popularly believed) merely something propositional, like knowledge or judgment. Truth is instead that which it describes. The matter itself is truth, meaning that a stated truth has a primordial connection with the thing (act, event, person, relationship) under consideration. Truth is what the thing shows of itself to the one who then articulates the truth shown. Among lawyers as among others, truth is a professional and communal thing. In that sense, lawyers submit to truths more so than they form, fashion, state, or discover them. Lawyers also help clients and others submit to those truths. If truth is professional and communal, then it requires of lawyers who will know it a special, participatory form of obedience. Truth will not accept outward conformity by convention but instead demands of lawyers an inward discerning and submitting by relatedness and reason.

> *Reflection*
> - Try asking students in class how they know something is true.
> - Then, through a sensitive Socratic examination, help them explore more deeply, what could, on reflection, prove to be a stock and unsatisfactory answer.
> - Then record and share with a colleague what you helped students learn about truth, knowledge, and thinking.

Prediction. Lawyers are also utterly dependent in their professional advice and service on their ability to predict. Law students might want to know why some lawyers are better at prediction than other lawyers are. Israel Scheffler showed how knowledge, truth, belief, evidence, reason, and justification (all critical to law and its practice) relate to education. Scheffler's starting point was knowledge's truth condition. For one to know something is not only to *personally* believe it but also requires that *others* (those who accept that the person knows it) *also* regard it as true.

Knowledge, in other words, has verifiable and predictive qualities. We know things not for comfort but because of their predictive value. Experience proves knowledge whether the knowledge is satisfying or not. Yet one cannot verify the truth condition of knowledge by experience. What one instead verifies is the accuracy of our declaration that we know. Lawyers can be right or wrong about truth. Experience will teach us. Yet truth remains true even if lawyers were wrong about its prediction. Therefore, lawyers must distinguish between *beliefs about* truth, which are important but subject to verification, and *truth itself*, which exists whether or not lawyers verify it. Experience cannot contradict truth. Experience instead always proves it.

Most lawyers respect statements about conditions and events because of the witness's experience. The best lawyers do so without giving up the solid ground of truth on which effective professional capacity and service depend. Consider, for example, a tort case involving a motor-vehicle collision. An eyewitness may testify to the circumstances of the collision, an expert may testify to injuries based on a medical record, and a law clerk may report the results of research on the law of the jurisdiction. These assertions would each represent verifiable beliefs about truths, not truths themselves. On the other hand, the medical condition of the plaintiff following the accident would constitute a truth, meaning an existing condition about which others may assert beliefs, whether those assertions are true or not. Lawyers recognize the difference. Law professors must help students do so. Your teaching vision can draw on deeper exploration of the basis for lawyer practices.

Skill. Law schools train students for law practice, not simply in law knowledge. How then do we relate knowledge to practice? Hungarian-British chemist Michael Polanyi showed how, for lawyers and other professionals, knowledge depends on practice. To *know* something can mean to be familiar with it, competent at it, comprehending of its truth, accepting of it as an article of faith, or valuing it as a normative judgment, for example. To *believe* something to be true suggests a propositional form of knowledge. One can reduce belief to the existence or non-existence of conditions or events. Knowledge, on the other hand, includes not only propositions (like beliefs) but also *procedures*, or what we might call *action logic*. While belief can be a source of and inspiration for knowledge, to *know* something further suggests procedural capability at it, meaning *practice* (in the law practice sense). Thus knowing depends on activity and experience, which together are the means by which students discover law knowledge and hold it to be true. Students cannot have knowledge without skill. Knowledge is use dependent.

> *Reflection*
> - Examine your course text from this standpoint. Reading between its lines, how does it represent knowledge?
> - Does it adequately reflect for students that knowledge is use dependent?
> - How does your syllabus encourage students to think about how lawyers use the knowledge that doctrine represents?

Practice. Polanyi also showed that like other experts, lawyers practice without explicitly thinking about the knowledge rules that their practice follows. (Lawyers think often and explicitly about legislated rules, not knowledge rules.) Lawyers examine and build upon their knowledge rules in reflective practice, but they do not employ those rules consciously in moment-to-moment action. Experts become self-conscious and paralyzed when focusing attention on an action's subsidiary elements. Skill is in that sense non-specifiable. Lawyers recover its fluency only by pouring themselves into their conceptual tools, assimilating them as part of their own identity. The concepts and doctrines with which a lawyer works must become extensions of the lawyer, whose whole identity the lawyer must devote to the skill's practice through active intention. For the lawyer, practice makes knowledge and skill into one entity, with the lawyer only vaguely aware of their separate existence.

Think of the implications of Polanyi's assertions for teaching either skills or doctrine. Consider the value of deepening your teaching vision by drawing on such sources. For example, following is a short list of instructional material and activities that might help students construct and acquire knowledge rules that readily transfer to law practice. After you read the list, see if you can generate a few others:

- law-practice vignettes included in course texts around the subject;

- study questions on practical strategies applying new knowledge;
- brief biographies of successful lawyers in the studied field;
- courtroom observation of lawyers practicing in the studied field; and
- practitioners speaking as classroom guests on the studied subject.

Purpose. Lawyers exercise their action knowledge, telling truths and making predictions, for special purposes. How can law students understand more about purpose? Swiss natural scientist Jean Piaget described two purposes for the way that knowledge controls actions. The first is to generate truths about situations and the second to construct creative solutions to those situations. The kind of truths lawyers tell is not solely the factual kind but also purposive and normative. Lawyers exercise a solving, restorative kind of creativity. When lawyers think, they do more than elaborate mental language mediated by logic and emotions. They connect client circumstances with truths held by relevant communities, truth itself being a communal property. Thinking and knowing carry with them purposes that we implicitly value.

Consider how such a teaching vision, centered on study of professional norms and purposes, might shape instruction. For example, analogical thinkers like lawyers draw on the intellectual norms of autonomy, entailment, inter-subjectivity, objectivity, and universality (recalled by the mnemonic AEIOU). Thus, lawyers are *autonomous* in their logic action, meaning that they think originally. Lawyers act autonomously when writing an opinion letter for an auditor on pending litigation. Lawyers also think about what situations should or must become, labeled *entailment*. Lawyers demonstrate entailment when drafting prayers for injunctive relief in complaint over public nuisances. Lawyers connect their thinking with the thinking of others, labeled *inter-subjectivity*. Lawyers demonstrate inter-subjectivity when responding paragraph by paragraph to an opposing lawyer's motion. Their thinking is *objective*, meaning that they connect it to verifiable truth. Lawyers show objectivity when evaluating whether to take a contingency-fee case. Lawyer thought is also *universal* in the Kantian sense that replicating it should lead to a desirable world. Lawyers act universally when they voluntarily disclose evidence in response to discovery requests, when others would not have discovered the evidence's concealment. Do you see how you could help students appreciate these professional norms through your instruction?

Ethics. Consider another example of teaching vision based on a study of ethics. Students cannot acquire the special forms of law knowledge suggested above without first having ethical identity. Russian psychologist Lev Vygotsky showed how identity forms through a combination of words, thoughts, and actions. Through psychological studies performed over a century ago, Vygotsky confirmed that words do not merely express knowledge. As a matter of scientifically demonstrated fact, we do not start with knowledge and move to its expression. Expression forms and shapes knowledge. Law professors should be interested to know that the actions of communicating influence what knowledge lawyers (and law students) form. The identity that we exhibit to others through our communication is not the product of our knowledge but an equal participant in creating it. Knowledge depends on ethical identity within relationship, meaning that for students to learn fully, they must develop full identity. Vygotsky also demonstrated that communication between two individuals often results in knowledge that neither communicator alone possessed, perhaps like a good cross-examination in which lawyer and witness together reveal knowledge neither previously held alone before the examination. How would such a revelation influence your instructional methods? These are just a few examples of how disciplined inquiry in other fields such as epistemology can contribute to teaching vision.

Conclusion. Ultimately, to teach is to care that learning happens. It is to foster student confidence in the ability to learn, attending to student needs, perhaps even by valuing them more than you value yourself, always being ready for service. Return to Parker Palmer and his earlier work *To Know as We Are Known*. Professor Palmer, who may be the most celebrated author writing on the higher-education teaching experience, had it right that first time (more so than in his subsequent *Courage to Teach*). The biblically literate will recognize his earlier title's reference, "to know as we are known," as coming from the apostle Paul's love chapter. That chapter identifies the self-sacrificial, caring-servant kind of love, not the sensual or filial love, as powerful, intense, and personified. Palmer found his vision and inspiration in ancient and trusted sources, and then drew on them in ways unique to his own identity, to touch and serve teachers and learners more broadly than he probably ever imagined. Do so likewise. Find the personified source of a power so pure and effective that its influence and presence through you will set students on fire with a passion for law. Find your unique identity and vision in the most essential thing that we all share, like commitment to the growth, learning, and well-being of one another.

Exercise 14

In an appropriately located electronic folder marked *Vision*, write brief answers to each of the following:

a. what are your clearest guiding principles for teaching, drawn from the deepest truths;

b. what are your most consistent practices related to teaching, connected to those truths; and

c. what are your most inspirational projects related to teaching, reflecting those truths.

Acknowledgments

I first acknowledge the debt that I owe to my colleagues and friends with whom I have taught over the past decade since the first edition of this book, for their patience, perseverance, balance, wisdom, and guidance. These law professors include especially David Tarrien, Tonya Krause-Phelan, Devin Schindler, Paul Sorensen, Victoria Vuletich, Marjorie Gell, Mike Molitor, Tracey Brame, Chris Hastings, Kim O'Leary, and Toree Randall. Development as a teacher depends on a community of scholars whose investigation of teaching stimulates one another.

I next acknowledge the support and steady character of the deans with whom I have administered and supported instruction over the past decade since the first edition of this book, including especially Chris Church, Amy Timmer, Joan Vestrand, Mike McDaniel, and Ron Sutton. Building a community of shared interests, collaboration, and trust, and maintaining a culture of discipline, teamwork, integrity, and respect, depends on wise managers with good hearts and the service ethic to commit them to the highest uses.

Finally, credit goes to the authors of the writings on law school, legal education, and higher education more generally, listed in the following bibliography. Nothing new appears in the above text. Although I based it in large part on my experience and experiences shared by colleagues, I also drew heavily from the rich teaching literature. Please permit this attribution to pay that substantial debt of gratitude.

Bibliography

ABA Section of Legal Education and Admissions to the Bar, *A Survey of Law School Curricula* (2012).

ABA SECTION OF LEGAL EDUCATION AND ADMISSIONS TO THE BAR, BEST PRACTICES REPORT ON THE USE OF ADJUNCT FACULTY (2011).

ABA Section of Legal Education and Admissions to the Bar, *Interim Report of the Outcome Measures Committee* (May 12, 2008).

ABA Section of Legal Education and Admissions to the Bar, *Legal Education and Professional Development—An Educational Continuum, Report of the Task Force on Law Schools and the Profession: Narrowing the Gap* (ABA 1992) (the "MacCrate Report").

ABA Section of Legal Education and Admissions to the Bar, *Standards for Approval of Law Schools* (ABA 2008-2009).

ABA Section of General Practice, General Practice Studies in Law Schools Committee, *Report on Lawyer Competencies* (1991).

ABA TASK FORCE ON LAWYER COMPETENCY, REPORT AND RECOMMENDATIONS: THE ROLE OF LAW SCHOOLS (1979).

ABA TASK FORCE ON THE FUTURE OF LEGAL EDUCATION, REPORT AND RECOMMENDATIONS (2014).

ABBOTT, IDA O., THE LAWYER'S GUIDE TO MENTORING (NALP 2000).

ALI-ABA, EQUIPPING OUR LAWYERS: LAW SCHOOL EDUCATION, CONTINUING LEGAL EDUCATION, AND LEGAL PRACTICE IN THE 21ST CENTURY (ALI-ABA 2009).

Ammar, Douglas B., *On Being Mentored in Law School: A Lawyer's Perspective*, 14 WIDENER L.J. 461 (2004-2005).

Angelo, Thomas Anthony, *Engaging and Supporting Faculty in the Scholarship of Assessment: Guidelines from Research and Best Practice*, in TRUDY W. BANTA AND ASSOCIATES, BUILDING A SCHOLARSHIP OF ASSESSMENT 191-194 (Jossey-Bass 2002).

Anzalone, Filippa M., *It All Begins with You: Improving Law School Learning Through Professional Self-Awareness and Critical Reflection*, 24 HAMLINE L.REV. 324, (2001).

Arredondo, Patricia, and Jeannette Gordon Reinoso, *Multicultural Competencies in Consultation*, in HANDBOOK OF MULTICULTURAL COMPETENCIES IN COUNSELING AND PSYCHOLOGY 330 (Sage Pub. 2003).

ARTHUR, JAMES, ED., CITIZENSHIP AND HIGHER EDUCATION—THE ROLE OF UNIVERSITIES IN COMMUNITIES AND SOCIETY (RoutledgeFalmer 2005).

Association of Am. Law Schools, *Report of the AALS Special Committee on Problems of Substance Abuse in the Law Schools*, 44 J. LEGAL EDUC. 35 (1994).

ASTIN, ALEXANDER W., AND HELEN S. ASTIN, LEADERSHIP RECONSIDERED: ENGAGING HIGHER EDUCATION IN SOCIAL CHANGE (W.K. Kellogg 2000).

Atkinson, Maxine P., *The Scholarship of Teaching and Learning: Reconceptualizing Scholarship and Transforming the Academy*, 79 SOCIAL FORCES 1217 (2001).

Australasian Professional Legal Education Council, Law Admissions Consultative Committee, *Competency Standards for Entry Level Lawyers* (Nov. 2000, updated Feb. 2002).

Bahls, Steven C., *Preparing General Practice Attorneys: Context-Based Lawyer Competencies*, 16 J. LEGAL PROF. 63 (1991).

Baker, Ronald L., *Keystones of Regional Accreditation: Intentions, Outcomes, and Sustainability*, in PETER HERNON & ROBERT E. DUGAN, EDS., OUTCOMES ASSESSMENT IN HIGHER EDUCATION 1 (Libraries Unlimited 2004).

BALL, ARNETHA F., MULTICULTURAL STRATEGIES FOR EDUCATION AND SOCIAL CHANGE: CARRIERS OF THE TORCH IN THE UNITED STATES AND SOUTH AFRICA (Teachers College Press 2006).

BARBER, DAVID, SURVIVING YOUR ROLE AS A LAWYER: A PROGRAM TO REDUCE STRESS AND INCREASE PRODUCTIVITY (Law Distribs. 1983).

Batt, Cynthia, and Harriet N. Katz, *Confronting Students: Evaluation in the Process of Mentoring Student Professional Development*, 10 CLINICAL L.REV. 581 (2003-2004).

Benchmark for Core Skills (First Draft), Palomar College (2007).

BERNSTEIN, DANIEL, AMY NELSON BURNETT, AMY GOODBURN, AND PAUL SAVORY, MAKING TEACHING AND LEARNING VISIBLE: COURSE PORTFOLIOS AND THE PEER REVIEW OF TEACHING 32 (Anker Pub. 2006).

BLOOM, BENJAMIN S., ED., TAXONOMY OF EDUCATIONAL OBJECTIVES, HANDBOOK 1: COGNITIVE DOMAIN (Addison Wesley Pub. Co., 1956).

Boice, Robert, *New Faculty as Teachers*, in KENNETH A. FELDMAN AND MICHAEL B. PAULSEN, TEACHING AND LEARNING IN THE COLLEGE CLASSROOM 241 (Pearson Custom Publishing 1998).

Brodie, Juliet M., *Post-Welfare Lawyering: Clinical Legal Education and a New Poverty Law Agenda*, 20 WASH. U. J.L. & POLY. 201 (2006).

BRITTON, BRUCE K., & ARTHUR C, GRAESSER, MODELS OF UNDERSTANDING TEXT (Lawrence Erlbaum Associates 1996).

BURHHART, ANN M., & ROBERT A. STEIN, LAW SCHOOL SUCCESS: A GUIDE TO STUDYING LAW AND TAKING LAW SCHOOL EXAMS 3RD ED. (West Academic Pub. 2017).

Burton, Angela Olivia, *Cultivating Ethical, Socially Responsible Lawyer Judgment: Introducing the Multiple Lawyering Intelligences Paradigm into the Clinical Setting*, 11 CLINICAL L. REV. 15 (2004).

BUTIN, DAN W., ED., SERVICE-LEARNING IN HIGHER EDUCATION (Palgrave MacMillan 2005).

Buttrey, Jeannette, and Nelson P. Miller, *Demonstrating and Contextualizing Legal Analysis* (co-author), in AMY TIMMER & NELSON MILLER, EDS., REFLECTIONS OF A LAWYER'S SOUL—THE INSTITUTIONAL EXPERIENCE OF PROFESSIONALISM AT THOMAS M. COOLEY LAW SCHOOL (William S. Hein & Co. 2008).

Bryant, Susan, *The Five Habits: Building Cross-Cultural Competence in Lawyers*, 8 CLIN. L. REV. 33 (2001).

CALLEROS, CHARLES R., LEGAL METHOD AND WRITING (Aspen Pubs. 2002).

CAMPOS, PAUL, DON'T GO TO LAW SCHOOL (UNLESS): A LAW PROFESSOR'S INSIDE GUIDE TO MAXIMIZING OPPORTUNITY AND MINIMIZING RISK (Campos 2012).

CARRINGTON, PAUL D., STEWARDS OF DEMOCRACY: LAW AS A PUBLIC PROFESSION (Westview Press 1999).

Carrington, Paul D., *Law as "The Common Thoughts of Men": The Law-Teaching and Judging of Thomas McIntyre Cooley*, 49 Stanford L.Rev. 495 (1997).

Cercone, Charles, and Nelson P. Miller, *Teaching Faculty How to Learn—Experiences in Faculty Development*, in AMY TIMMER & NELSON MILLER, EDS., REFLECTIONS OF A LAWYER'S SOUL—THE INSTITUTIONAL EXPERIENCE OF PROFESSIONALISM AT THOMAS M. COOLEY LAW SCHOOL (William S. Hein & Co. 2008).

CHARLES, C.M., INTRODUCTION TO EDUCATIONAL RESEARCH (Longman 3d. ed. 1998).

Christensen, Leah M., *The Paradox of Legal Expertise: A Study of Experts and Novices Reading the Law*, 2008 B.Y.U. L.REV. 53.

Christensen, Leah M., *The Psychology Behind Case Briefing: A Powerful Cognitive Schema*, 29 CAMPBELL L.REV. 5 (2006).

CLAXTON, CHARLES S., & PATRICIA H. MURRELL, LEARNING STYLES: IMPLICATIONS FOR IMPROVING EDUCATIONAL PRACTICES (Association for the Study of Higher Education 1987).

Chen, James R., Michael V. Fortunato, Alan Mandell, Susan Oaks, and Duncan RyanMann, *Reconceptualizing the Faculty Role: Alternative Models*, in BARBARA LEIGH SMITH & JOHN MCCANN, EDS., REINVENTING OURSELVES—INTERDISCIPLINARY EDUCATION, COLLABORATIVE LEARNING, AND EXPERIMENTATION IN HIGHER EDUCATION 328 (Anker Publishing 2001).

COLBY, ANNE, ELIZABETH BEAUMONT, THOMAS EHRLICH, & JOSH CORNGOLD, EDUCATING FOR DEMOCRACY—PREPARING UNDERGRADUATES FOR RESPONSIBLE POLITICAL ENGAGEMENT (Jossey-Bass 2007).

Coleman, Hardin L.K., and Donald B. Pope-Davis, *Integrating Multicultural Counseling Theory*, in DONALD R. POPE-DAVIS AND HARDIN L.K. COLEMAN, EDS., THE INTERSECTION OF RACE, CLASS, AND GENDER IN MULTICULTURAL COUNSELING ix (Sage Pubs. 2001).

Coleman, Steven R., *Dangerous Outposts: Progressive Experiments in Higher Education in the 1920s and 1930s*, in BARBARA LEIGH SMITH & JOHN MCCANN, EDS., REINVENTING OURSELVES—INTERDISCIPLINARY EDUCATION, COLLABORATIVE LEARNING, AND EXPERIMENTATION IN HIGHER EDUCATION 6 (Anker Publishing 2001).

Constantine, Madonna G., and Derald Wing Sue, *The American Psychological Association's Guidelines on Multicultural Education, Training, Research, Practice, and Organizational Psychology: Initial Development and Summary*, in MADONNA G. CONSTANTINE AND DERALD WING SUE, STRATEGIES FOR BUILDING MULTICULTURAL COMPETENCE IN MENTAL HEALTH AND EDUCATIONAL SETTINGS 3 (John Wiley & Sons 2005).

COOPER, DAVID D., ED., TRYING THE TIES THAT BIND—ESSAYS ON SERVICE-LEARNING AND MORAL LIFE OF FACULTY (Fetzer Institute 2000).

Cox, Milton D., *The Role of Community in Learning—Making Connections for Your Classroom and Campus, Your Students and Colleagues*, in GARY S. WHEELER, ED., TEACHING & LEARNING IN COLLEGE 10 (Info-Tec 2002).

Cross, K. Patricia, *Classroom Research: Helping Professors Learn More About Teaching and Learning*, in PETER SELDIN, HOW ADMINISTRATORS CAN IMPROVE TEACHING 128 (Jossey-Bass 1990).

CURRIER, KATHERINE A., & THOMAS E. EIMERMANN, THE STUDY OF LAW: A CRITICAL THINKING APPROACH 3RD ED. (Wolters Kluwer 2013).

D'Andrea, Michael, and Judy Daniels, *Respectful Counseling: An Integrative Multidimensional Model for Counselors*, in DONALD R. POPE-DAVIS AND HARDIN L.K. COLEMAN, EDS., THE INTERSECTION OF RACE, CLASS, AND GENDER IN MULTICULTURAL COUNSELING 417 (Sage Pubs. 2001).

Daggett, Lynn M., *All of the Above: Computerized Exam Scoring of Multiple Choice Items Helps to: (A) Show How Exam Items Worked Technically, (B) Maximize Exam Fairness, (C) Justly Assign Letter Grades, and (D) Provide Feedback on Student Learning*, 57 J. LEGAL EDUC. 391 (2007).

DAICOFF, SUSAN, LAWYER KNOW THYSELF: A PSYCHOLOGICAL ANALYSIS OF PERSONALITY STRENGTHS AND WEAKNESSES (American Psychological Assn. 2004).

Daicoff, Susan, *Lawyer, Know Thyself: A Review of Empirical Research on Attorney Attributes Bearing on Professionalism*, 46 AM. U. L.REV. 1337 (1997).

DAVIS, BARBARA GROSS, TOOLS FOR TEACHING (2d ed. Jossey-Bass 2009).

Delgado-Romero, Edward A., Jessica Barfield, Benetta Fairley, and Rebecca S. Martinez, *Using the Multicultural Guidelines in Individual and Group Counseling Situations*, in MADONNA G. CONSTANTINE AND DERALD WING SUE, STRATEGIES FOR BUILDING MULTICULTURAL COMPETENCE IN MENTAL HEALTH AND EDUCATIONAL SETTINGS 39 (John Wiley & Sons 2005).

DENNING, BRANNON P., MARCIA L. MCCORMICK, & JEFFREY M. LIPSHAW, BECOMING A LAW PROFESSOR: A CANDIDATE'S GUIDE (ABA Publishing 2010).

DEWEY, JOHN, EXPERIENCE AND EDUCATION (MacMillan Co. 1938).

DEWEY, JOHN, HOW WE THINK (D.C. Heath & Co. 1933).

deWinstanley, Patricia A., and Robert A. Bjork, *Successful Lecturing: Presenting Information in Ways that Engage Effective Processing*, in DIANE F. HALPERN AND MILTON D. HAKEL, APPLYING THE SCIENCE OF LEARNING TO UNIVERSITY TEACHING AND BEYOND (Jossey-Bass 2002).

Dewitz, Peter, *Legal Education: A Problem of Learning from Text*, 23 N.Y.U. REV. L. & SOC. CHANGE 235 (1997).

DIAMOND, ROBERT M., DESIGNING AND ASSESS COURSES AND CURRICULA: A PRACTICAL GUIDE (Jossey-Bass, 1997).

Diamond, Robert M., *Faculty, Instructional, and Organizational Development: Options and Choices*, in KAY HERR GILLESPIE, ED., A GUIDE TO FACULTY DEVELOPMENT: PRACTICAL ADVICE, EXAMPLES, AND RESOURCES 2 (Anker Pub. Co. 2002).

DICK, WALTER, AND LOU CAREY, THE SYSTEMATIC DESIGN OF INSTRUCTION (4th ed. HarperCollins 1996).

Dirkx, John M., *Authenticity and Imagination*, in PATRICIA CRANTON, NEW DIRECTIONS FOR ADULT AND CONTINUING EDUCATION 27 (Jossey-Bass 2006).

Dressel, Paul L., and Dora Marcus, *Teaching Styles and Effects on Learning*, in KENNETH A. FELDMAN AND MICHAEL B. PAULSEN, TEACHING AND LEARNING IN THE COLLEGE CLASSROOM 495 (Pearson Custom Publishing 1998).

DROGE, DAVID, & BREN ORTEGA MURPHY, EDS., VOICES OF STRONG DEMOCRACY—CONCEPTS AND MODELS FOR SERVICE LEARNING IN COMMUNICATION STUDIES (American Association for Higher Education 1999).

EADES, RONALD W., HOW TO BE A LAW PROFESSOR: FROM GETTING THAT FIRST JOB TO RETIREMENT (Vandeplas Pub. 2008).

Edgerton, Russell, Patricia Hutchings, & Kathleen Quinlan, *The Teaching Portfolio*, in KENNETH A. FELDMAN AND MICHAEL B. PAULSEN, TEACHING AND LEARNING IN THE COLLEGE CLASSROOM 675 (Pearson Custom Publishing 1998).

Evensen, Dorothy H., James F. Stratman, Laurel C. Oates, & Sarah Zappe, *Developing an Assessment of First-Year Law Students' Critical Case Reading and Reasoning Ability: Phase 2* (Law School Admission Council 2009).

Ewell, Peter T., *An Emerging Scholarship: A Brief History of Assessment*, in TRUDY W. BANTA AND ASSOCIATES, BUILDING A SCHOLARSHIP OF ASSESSMENT 22 (Jossey-Bass 2002).

FARNSWORTH, KENT A., LEADERSHIP AS SERVICE—A NEW MODEL FOR HIGHER EDUCATION IN A NEW CENTURY (American Council on Higher Education 2007).

FINK, L. DEE, CREATING SIGNIFICANT LEARNING EXPERIENCES: AN INTEGRATED APPROACH TO DESIGNING COLLEGE COURSES (Jossey-Bass 2003).

Fincher, Cameron, *Learning Theory and Research*, in KENNETH A. FELDMAN & MICHAEL B. PAULSEN, TEACHING AND LEARNING IN THE COLLEGE CLASSROOM 57 (2d ed. Pearson Custom Pub. 1998).

FINES, BARBARA GLESNER, LAW SCHOOL MATERIALS FOR SUCCESS (CALI eLangdell Press 2013).

Finkel, Donald L., *Should the Teacher Know the Anwer? Two Ways to Organize Interdisciplinary Study Around Inquiry*, in BARBARA LEIGH SMITH & JOHN MCCANN, EDS., REINVENTING OURSELVES—INTERDISCIPLINARY EDUCATION, COLLABORATIVE LEARNING, AND EXPERIMENTATION IN HIGHER EDUCATION 212 (Anker Publishing 2001).

FJERSTAD, JESSICA L., LEGAL EDUCAITON: THE PREPARATION OF LAW STUDENTS FOR THE LEGAL PROFESSION (Honors thesis 2008).

Forsyth, Donelson R., & James H. McMillan, *Practical Proposals for Motivating Students*, in KENNETH A. FELDMAN AND MICHAEL B. PAULSEN, TEACHING AND LEARNING IN THE COLLEGE CLASSROOM 551 (Pearson Custom Publishing 1998).

FOSTER, STEVE, HOW TO WRITE BETTER LAW ESSAYS 4TH ED. (Pearson 2016).

FOX, HELEN, "WHEN RACE BREAKS OUT"—CONVERSATIONS ABOUT RACE AND RACISM IN COLLEGE CLASSROOMS (Peter Lang Publishing, Inc. 2001).

Frank, Judith, Gina Torielli, and Nelson P. Miller, *To Think, to Act, to Learn: From Process to Performance*, in AMY TIMMER & NELSON MILLER, EDS., REFLECTIONS OF A LAWYER'S SOUL—THE INSTITUTIONAL EXPERIENCE OF PROFESSIONALISM AT THOMAS M. COOLEY LAW SCHOOL (William S. Hein & Co. 2008).

Frego, Katherine A., *Authenticity and Relationships with Students*, in PATRICIA CRANTON, NEW DIRECTIONS FOR ADULT AND CONTINUING EDUCATION 41 (Jossey-Bass 2006).

Furhmann, Barbara Schneider, and Anthony F. Grasha, *The Past, Present, and Future in College Teaching: Where Does Your Teaching Fit?*, KENNETH A. FELDMAN & MICHAEL B. PAULSEN, TEACHING AND LEARNING IN THE COLLEGE CLASSROOM 5 (Pearson Custom Publishing 2d ed. 1994).

GAGNE, ROBERT, ESSENTIALS OF LEARNING FOR INSTRUCTION (The Dryden Press 1974).

GAGNE, ROBERT M., THE CONDITIONS OF LEARNING AND THEORY OF INSTRUCTION (4th ed. Holt, Rinehart & Winston 1985).

GALBENSKI, DAVID, UNBOUND: HOW ENTREPRENEURSHIP IS DRAMATICALLY TRANSFORMING LEGAL SERVICES TODAY (CIS CUSTOM PUB. 2009).

GANNON, MARTIN J., CULTURAL METAPHORS: READINGS, RESEARCH TRANSLATIONS, AND COMMENTARY (Sage Pubs. 2000).

GARRETSON, HEATHER, & NELSON P. MILLER, *Preserving Law School's Signature Pedagogy and Great Subjects*, 88/5 MICHIGAN BAR JOURNAL 46 (2009).

Garvey, John Burwell, & Anne F. Zinkin, *Making Law Students Client-Ready: A New Model in Legal Education*, 102 DUKE FORUM FOR LAW & SOC. CHANGE 101 (2009).

GLASS, KATHY TUCHMAN, CURRICULUM MAPPING—A STEP-BY-STEP GUIDE FOR CREATING CURRICULUM YEAR OVERVIEWS (Corwin Press 2007).

Gloria, Alberta M., *The Cultural Construction of Latinas*, in DONALD R. POPE-DAVIS AND HARDIN L.K. COLEMAN, EDS., THE INTERSECTION OF RACE, CLASS, AND GENDER IN MULTICULTURAL COUNSELING 3 (Sage Pubs. 2001).

GOTTLIEB, KARLA, & GAIL ROBINSON, A PRACTICAL GUIDE FOR INTEGRATING CIVIC RESPONSIBILITY INTO THE CURRICULUM (Community College Press 2002).

GRISE, JANE BLOOM, CRITICAL READING FOR SUCCESS IN LAW SCHOOL AND BEYOND (West Academic Pub. 2017).

Hall, Gordon C.N., Irene R. Lopez, and Anita Bansal, *Academic Acculturation: Race, Gender, and Class Issues*, in DONALD R. POPE-DAVIS AND HARDIN L.K. COLEMAN, EDS., THE INTERSECTION OF RACE, CLASS, AND GENDER IN MULTICULTURAL COUNSELING 171 (Sage Pubs. 2001).

HANOVER RESEARCH COUNCIL, INTEGRATING PRACTICAL SKILLS INTO THE LAW SCHOOL CURRICULUM (Hanover 2010).

HASEN, RICHARD L., THE GLANNON GUIDE TO TORTS: LEARNING TORTS THROUGH MULTIPLE-CHOICE QUESTIONS AND ANALYSIS (Wolters Kluwer 2009).

Hawke, Constance, *Tenure's Tenacity in Higher Education*, 120 Ed. Law Rep. 621 (1997).

HEATH, MARILYN S., ELECTRONIC PORTFOLIOS: A GUIDE TO PROFESSIONAL DEVELOPMENT AND ASSESSMENT (Linworth Publishing 2004).

HEIDEGGER, MARTIN, BEING AND TIME (State Univ. of New York Press 1996) (Joan Stambaugh, trans.).

Henderson, Bethany R., *Asking the Lost Question: What Is the Purpose of Law School?*, 53 J. LEGAL EDUC. 48 (2003).

HESS, GERALD F., STEVEN I. FRIEDLAND, MICHAEL HUNTER SCHWARTZ, & SOPHIE SPARROW, TECHNIQUES FOR TEACHING LAW 2 (Carolina Academic Press 2011).

Hofstede, Geert, and Michael H. Bond, *The Confucius Connection: From Cultural Roots to Economic Growth*, in GANNON, MARTIN J., CULTURAL METAPHORS: READINGS, RESEARCH TRANSLATIONS, AND COMMENTARY 31 (Sage Pubs. 2000).

Humber, Toni-Mokjaetji, *Intercultural Adaptations: A Stranger but Not Strange*, in MILLHOUSE, VIRGINIA H., MOLEFI K. ASANTE, AND PETER O. NWOSU, TRANSCULTURAL REALITIES: INTERDISCIPLINARY PERSPECTIVES ON CROSS-CULTURAL RELATIONS 227 (Sage Pubs. 2001).

Hutchings, Pat, *Defining Features and Significant Functions of the Course Portfolio*, in PAT HUTCHINGS, ED., THE COURSE PORTFOLIO: HOW FACULTY CAN EXAMINE THEIR TEACHING TO ADVANCE PRACTICE AND IMPROVE STUDENT LEARNING 24 (AAHE 1998).

HOLLAND, JAMES A., AND JULIAN S. WEBB, LEARNING LEGAL RULES: A STUDENT'S GUIDE TO LEGAL METHOD AND REASONING (Blackstone Press Ltd. 1993).

ISRAEL, SUSAN E., AND CYNTHIA A. LASSONDE, EDS., THE ETHICAL EDUCATOR—INTEGRATING ETHICS WITHIN THE CONTEXT OF TEACHING AND TEACHER RESEARCH (Peter Lang Pub. 2007).

Johnson, Annette B., *Current Trends in Faculty Personnel Policies: Appointment, Evaluation and Termination*, 44 ST. LOUIS U. L.J. 81 (2000).

JOHNSON, BRIAN T., & CAROLYN R. O'GRADY, EDS., THE SPIRIT OF SERVICE—EXPLORING FAITH, SERVICE, AND SOCIAL JUSTICE IN HIGHER EDUCATION (Anker Publishing 2006).

JOSEPHSON, MICHAEL, LEARNING AND EVALUATION IN LAW SCHOOL (AALS 1984).

Jackson, Lisa R., *The Interaction of Race and Gender in African American Women's Experiences of Self and Other at a Predominantly White Women's College*, in DONALD R. POPE-DAVIS AND HARDIN L.K. COLEMAN, EDS., THE INTERSECTION OF RACE, CLASS, AND GENDER IN MULTICULTURAL COUNSELING 49 (Sage Pubs. 2001).

KALLICK, BENA, AND JEFF COLOSIMO, USING CURRICULUM MAPPING & ASSESSMENT DATA TO IMPROVE LEARNING 52 (Corwin Press 2009).

KAUFMAN, GEORGE W., THE LAWYER'S GUIDE TO BALANCING LIFE AND WORK—TAKING THE STRESS OUT OF SUCCESS (ABA 1999).

KECSKES, KEVIN, ED., ENGAGING DEPARTMENTS—MOVING FACULTY CULTURE FROM PRIVATE TO PUBLIC, INDIVIDUAL TO COLLECTIVE FOCUS FOR THE COMMON GOOD (Anker Publishing 2006).

KEELING, RICHARD P., ED., LEARNING RECONSIDERED: A CAMPUS-WIDE FOCUS ON THE STUDENT EXPERIENCE (ACPA/NASPA 2004).

Kim, Min-Sun, *Perspectives on Human Communication: Implications for Transculture Theory*, in MILLHOUSE, VIRGINIA H., MOLEFI K. ASANTE, AND PETER O. NWOSU, TRANSCULTURAL REALITIES: INTERDISCIPLINARY PERSPECTIVES ON CROSS-CULTURAL RELATIONS 3 (Sage Pubs. 2001).

KIMBALL, BRUCE A., THE INCEPTION OF MODERN PROFESSIONAL EDUCATION: C.C. LANGDELL 1926-1906 (University of North Carolina Press 2009).

KISSAM, PHILIP C., THE DISCIPLINE OF LAW SCHOOLS: THE MAKING OF MODERN LAWYERS (Carolina Academic Press 2003).

KRATHWOHL, D.R., AND BENJAMIN S. BLOOM, & B.B. MASIA, TAXONOMY OF EDUCATIONAL OBJECTIVES, THE CLASSIFICATION OF EDUCATIONAL GOALS. HANDBOOK II: AFFECTIVE DOMAIN (David McKay Co. 1973).

KUNDA, ZIVA, SOCIAL COGNITION: MAKING SENSE OF PEOPLE (MIT Press 1999).

Lakoff, George, and Mark Johnson, *Metaphors We Live By*, in GANNON, MARTIN J., CULTURAL METAPHORS: READINGS, RESEARCH TRANSLATIONS, AND COMMENTARY 3 (Sage Pubs. 2000).

Law School Survey of Student Engagement (LSSSE), *Student Engagement in Law School: Enhancing Student Learning* (2009 Annual Survey Results).

Law School Survey of Student Engagement (LSSSE), *Student Engagement in Law School: Preparing 21st Century Lawyers* (2008 Annual Survey Results).

LEBLANC, ADRIAN N., RANDOM FAMILY: LOVE, DRUGS, TROUBLE, AND COMING OF AGE IN THE BRONX (Scribner 2003).

LE BRUN, MARGARET, & RICHARD JOHNSTONE, THE QUIET REVOLUTION—IMPROVING STUDENT LEARNING IN LAW 88 (The Law Book Co. 1994).

LENNING, OSCAR T., AND LARRY H. EBBERS, THE POWERFUL POTENTIAL OF LEARNING COMMUNITIES (ASHE-ERIC 1999).

Leong, Frederick T.L., and Aditya Bhagwat, *Challenges in "Unpacking" the Universal, Group, and Individual Dimensions of Cross-Cultural Counseling and Psychotherapy: Openness to Experience as a Critical Dimension*, in DONALD R. POPE-DAVIS AND HARDIN L.K. COLEMAN, EDS., THE INTERSECTION OF RACE, CLASS, AND GENDER IN MULTICULTURAL COUNSELING 241 (Sage Pubs. 2001).

LE VAN, GERALD, LAWYERS' LIVES OUT OF CONTROL: A QUALITY OF LIFE HANDBOOK (Worldcomm Press 1992).

LITOWITZ, DOUGLAS, THE DESTRUCTION OF YOUNG LAWYERS: BEYOND ONE L (Univ. of Akron Press 2006).

LOPEZ, JIM V., THE FUNDAMENTALS OF LAW SCHOOL: SURVIVAL STRATEGIES FOR LAW STUDENTS (Anvil Publishing 2012).

Lowman, Joseph, *What Constitutes Masterful Teaching*, in KENNETH A. FELDMAN AND MICHAEL B. PAULSEN, TEACHING AND LEARNING IN THE COLLEGE CLASSROOM 503 (Pearson Custom Publishing 1998).

Liu, William M., *Expanding Our Understanding of Multiculturalism: Developing a Social Class Worldview Model*, in DONALD R. POPE-DAVIS AND HARDIN L.K. COLEMAN, EDS., THE INTERSECTION OF RACE, CLASS, AND GENDER IN MULTICULTURAL COUNSELING 127 (Sage Pubs. 2001).

LLEWELLYN, KARL N., THE BRAMBLE BUSH (Oxford Univ. Press 2008) (original copyright 1930).

Lloyd, Harold Anthony, Theory Without Practice Is Empty; Practice Without Theory Is Blind: The Inherent Inseparability of Doctrine and Skills, in LINDA H. EDWARDS, THE DOCTRINE/SKILLS DIVIDE: LEGAL EDUCATION'S SELF-INFLICTED WOUND 77-90 (2017).

Lundeberg, Mary A., *Metacognitive Aspects of Reading Comprehension: Studying Understanding in Legal Case Analysis*, 22 READING RES. Q. 407 (1987).

Lyons, Nona, *Advancing the Scholarship of Teaching and Learning: Reflective Portfolio Inquiry in Higher Education—a Case Study of One Institution*, 22 IRISH EDUC. STUDIES 69 (2003).

MACFARLANE, BRUCE, THE ACADEMIC CITIZEN—THE VIRTUE OF SERVICE IN UNIVERSITY LIFE (Routledge 2007).

MACGREGOR, JEAN, ED., INTEGRATING LEARNING COMMUNITIES WITH SERVICE-LEARNING (American Association for Higher Education 2003).

MADDEN, STEVEN J., ED., SERVICE LEARNING ACROSS THE CURRICULUM—CASE APPLICATIONS IN HIGHER EDUCATION (University Press of America 2000).

MAGER, ROBERT F., & PETER PIPE, ANALYZING PERFORMANCE PROBLEMS, 3RD ED. (Center for Effective Performance 1997).

MAGER, ROBERT F., GOAL ANALYSIS: HOW TO CLARIFY YOUR GOALS SO YOU CAN ACTUALLY ACHIEVE THEM, 3RD ED. (Center for Effective Performance 1997).

MAGER, ROBERT F., HOW TO TURN LEARNERS ON… WITHOUT TURNING THEM OFF (Center for Effective Performance 1997).

MAGER, ROBERT F., MAKING INSTRUCTION WORK: A STEP-BY-STEP GUIDE TO DESIGNING AND DEVELOPING INSTRUCTION THAT WORKS, 2ND ED. (Center for Effective Performance 1997).

MAGER, ROBERT F., MEASURING INSTRUCTIONAL RESULTS, OR GOT A MATCH? 3D ED. (Center for Effective Performance 1997).

MAGER, ROBERT F., PREPARING INSTRUCTIONAL OBJECTIVES: A CRITICAL TOOL IN THE DEVELOPMENT OF EFFECTIVE INSTRUCTION (Center for Effective Performance 1997).

MAHARG, PAUL, TRANSFORMING LEGAL EDUCATION—LEARNING AND TEACHING LAW IN THE EARLY TWENTY-FIRST CENTURY (Ashgate 2007).

Maki, Peggy L., *Developing an Assessment Plan to Learn About Student Learning*, in PETER HERNON & ROBERT E. DUGAN, EDS., OUTCOMES ASSESSMENT IN HIGHER EDUCATION 89 (Libraries Unlimited 2004).

MARANVILLE, DEBORAH, LISA RADTKE BLISS, CAROLYN WILKES KAAS, & ANTOINETTE SEDILLO LOPEZ, EDS., BUILDING ON BEST PRACTICES: TRANSFORMING LEGAL EDUCATION IN A CHANGING WORLD (LexisNexis 2015).

MART, SUSAN NEVELOW, ED., THE BOULDER STATEMENTS ON LEGAL RESEARCH EDUCATION: THE INTERSECTION OF INTELLECTUAL AND PRACTICAL SKILLS (William S. Hein & Co. 2014).

MARTIN, Joanne, and Bryant G. Garth, *Clinical Education as a Bridge Between Law School and Practice: Mitigating the Misery*, 1 CLINICAL L. REV. 443 (1994).

Mason, L. John, *Optimal Performance for Lawyers* in JULIE M. TAMMINEN, ED., LIVING WITH THE LAW: STRATEGIES TO AVOID BURNOUT AND CREATE BALANCE 23 (ABA 1997).

Matasar, Richard A., *Skills and Values Education: Debate About the Continuum Continues*, 19 N.Y.L. SCHO. J. HUM. RTS. 25 (2003).

Mayer, Richard E., & Merlin C. Wittrock, *Problem Solving*, in PATRICIA A. ALEXANDER & PHILIP H. WINNE, HANDBOOK OF EDUCATIONAL PSYCHOLOGY 289 (Lawrence Erlbaum Assocs. Pubs. 2nd ed. 2006).

MCCRAY, NIYA T., SURVIVING LAW SCHOOL: A GUIDE ON HOW TO BALANCE THE SCALES (2017).

McKeachie, Wilbert J., Teaching Tips—A Guidebook for the Beginning College Teacher (7th ed. D.C. Heath & Co. 1978).

McKeachie, Wilbert J., Teaching Tips—Strategies, Research, and Theory for College and University Teachers (10th ed. Houghton Mifflin Co.).

McKeachie, Wilbert J., Paul R. Pintrich, Yi-Guang Lin, David A.F. Smith, & Rajeev Sharma, Teaching and Learning in the College Classroom—A Review of the Research Literature (Univ. of Michigan Press 1986).

McKeachie, Wilbert J., *Research on College Teaching: The Historical Background*, in Kenneth A. Feldman & Michael B. Paulsen, Teaching and Learning in the College Classroom 26 (2d ed. Pearson Custom Pub. 1998).

McKenna, Michael C., & Richard D. Robinson, Teaching Through Text: Reading and Writing in the Content Areas (Pearson Education Inc. 4th ed. 2006).

McKinney, Ruth Ann, Reading Like a Lawyer—Time-Saving Strategies for Reading Law Like an Expert 2nd ed. (Carolina Academic Press 2012).

McNeil, Heidi L., *Problems Identified: The Bar Surveys* in Jeffrey R. Simmons, Ed., Life, Law and the Pursuit of Balance: A Lawyer's Guide to Quality of Life 9 (ABA/ Maricopa County Bar Assn. 1997).

Merritt, Deborah Jones, *Dodging Bulletts: PowerPoint for Law Professors* (unpublished paper 2005).

Mertz, Elizabeth, *Teaching Lawyers the Language of Law: Legal and Anthropological Translations*, 34 J. Marshall L. Rev. 91 (2000).

Mertz, Elizabeth, The Language of Law School—Learning to Think Like a Lawyer (2007).

Millhouse, Virginia H., Molefi K. Asante, and Peter O. Nwosu, Transcultural Realities: Interdisciplinary Perspectives on Cross-Cultural Relations ix (Sage Pubs. 2001).

Miller, Nelson P., A Law Graduate's Guide—Navigating Law School's Hidden Career and Professional Development Curriculum (Bridge Publishing Co. 2011).

Miller, Nelson P., A Law Student's Guide—Legal Education's Knowledge, Skills, and Ethics Dimensions (Carolina Academic Press 2010).

Miller, Nelson P., *An Apprenticeship of Professional Identity—A Paradigm for Educating Lawyers*, 87 Mich. Bar J. 20 (2008).

Miller, Nelson P., *Beyond Bias: Cultural Competence as a Lawyer Skill*, 87/6 Michigan Bar Journal 38 (2008).

Miller, Nelson P., Dear J.D.: What to Do with Your Law Degree (Crown Mgt. 2014).

Miller, Nelson P., Going to Law School: Preparing for a Transformative Experience (Crown Mgt. 2016).

Miller, Nelson P., *Instruction in Meta-Ethical Competence*, in Amy Timmer & Nelson Miller, eds., Reflections of a Lawyer's Soul—The Institutional Experience of Professionalism at Thomas M. Cooley Law School (William S. Hein & Co. 2008).

Miller, Nelson P., and Douglas A. Johnson, Preparing for the Bar Exam: Plans, Programs, Content, Conditions, and Skills (Crown Mgt. 2015).

Miller, Nelson P., Civil Procedure in Practice, Volume II: Adjudication Process & Result (2nd ed. Vandeplas 2015).

Miller, Nelson P., and Tonya Krause-Phelan, Preparing for the Multistate Bar Examination, Volume I: Multiple-Choice Strategies and Multiple-Choice Questions, Answers, and Explanations for Every MBE Topic and Subtopic (All Subjects) (Crown Mgt. 2017).

Miller, Nelson P., and Tonya Krause-Phelan, Preparing for the Multistate Bar Examination, Volume II: Multiple-Choice Strategies and Multiple-Choice Questions, Answers, and Explanations for Every MBE Topic and Subtopic (MBE Subjects Separated Into Seven 100-Question Banks) (Crown Mgt. 2017).

Miller, Nelson P., Preparing for the Multistate Bar Examination, Volume III: An Outline of Every MBE Topic and Subtopic (Crown Mgt. 2017).

MILLER, NELSON P., CHARLES P. CERCONE, AND CHRISTOPHER TRUDEAU, TEACHING LAW PRACTICE: PREPARING THE NEXT GENERATION OF LAWYERS (Vandeplas Pub. 2013).

MILLER, NELSON P., PAUL T. SORENSEN, KAREN L. CHADWICK, AND MONICA R. NUCKOLLS, THE PRACTICE OF TORT LAW (Vandeplas Publishing Co. 3rd ed. 2010).

MILLER, NELSON P., AND VICTORIA VULETICH, THE LAW, PRINCIPLES, AND PRACTICE OF LEGAL ETHICS (Vandeplas Publishing Co. 2nd ed. 2012).

Mio, Jeffrey S., *On Teaching Multiculturalism: History, Models, and Content*, in GUILLERMO BERNAL, JOSEPH TRIMBLE, A. KATHLEEN BURLEW, AND FREDERICK LEONG, HANDBOOK OF RACIAL & ETHNIC MINORITY PYSCHOLOGY 119-120 (Sage Pub. 2003).

Mollen, Debra, Charles R. Ridley, and Carrie L. Hill, *Models of Multicultural Counseling Competence*, in HANDBOOK OF MULTICULTURAL COMPETENCIES IN COUNSELING AND PSYCHOLOGY 21 (Sage Pub. 2003).

Monk, Carl C., & Harry G. Prince, *How Can an Association of Law Schools Promote Quality Legal Education?*, 43 S. TEX. L.REV. 507 (2002).

MOSKOVITZ, GORDON B., SOCIAL COGNITION: UNDERSTANDING SELF AND OTHERS (Guilford Press 2005).

MOSS, DAVID M., & DEBRA MOSS CURTIS, EDS., REFORMING LEGAL EDUCATION: LAW SCHOOLS AT THE CROSSROADS (Information Age Pub., Inc. 2012).

MULDOON, GARY, THE EDUCATION OF A LAWYER: ESSENTIAL SKILLS AND UNCOMMON ADVICE FOR BUILDING A SUCCESSFUL CAREER (ABA Publishing 2015).

Munro, Gregory S., *How Do We Know If We Are Achieving Our Goals?: Strategies for Assessing the Outcome of Curricular Innovation*, 1 J. ASSN. LEGAL WRITING DIRECTORS 229 (2004).

Myers, Linda J., Ezemenari M. Obasi, Monica Jefferson, Michelle Anderson, Tamara Godfrey, and Jason Purnell, *Building Multicultural Competence Around Indigenous Healing Practices*, in MADONNA G. CONSTANTINE AND DERALD WING SUE, STRATEGIES FOR BUILDING MULTICULTURAL COMPETENCE IN MENTAL HEALTH AND EDUCATIONAL SETTINGS 109 (John Wiley & Sons 2005).

NADVORNEY, DAVID, & DEBORAH ZALESNE, TEACHING TO EVERY STUDENT: EXPLICITLY INTEGRATING SKILLS AND THEORY INTO THE CONTRACTS CLASS (Carolina Academic Press 2013).

Newell, William H., *Powerful Pedagogies*, in BARBARA LEIGH SMITH & JOHN MCCANN, EDS., REINVENTING OURSELVES—INTERDISCIPLINARY EDUCATION, COLLABORATIVE LEARNING, AND EXPERIMENTATION IN HIGHER EDUCATION 196 (Anker Publishing 2001).

NOREIUL, CHAD, LAW 101: WHAT LAW SCHOOL'S *REALLY* LIKE (Carolina Academic Press 2015).

Oates, Laurel Currie, *Beating the Odds: Reading Strategies of Law Students Admitted Through Alternative Admissions Programs*, 83 IOWA L. REV. 139 (1997).

O'Leary, Kim, Nelson Miller, Tracey Brame, and Dale Iverson, *Cultural Competence as a Professional Skill*, in AMY TIMMER AND NELSON MILLER, EDS., REFLECTIONS OF A LAWYER'S SOUL—THE INSTITUTIONAL EXPERIENCE OF PROFESSIONALISM AT THOMAS M. COOLEY LAW SCHOOL (William S. Hein & Co. 2008).

O'Leary, Kim, Nelson P. Miller, Tracey Brame, and Goldie Adele, *Equality as Talisman: Getting Beyond Bias to Cultural Competence as a Professional Skill*, 25 COOLEY L. REV. 100 (2008).

OLSON, KURT, & LAWRENCE R. VELVEL, THE GATHERING PEASANTS' REVOLT IN AMERICAN LEGAL EDUCATION (Douksan Press 2008).

Ortony, Andrew, *Why Metaphors Are Necessary and Not Just Nice*, in GANNON, MARTIN J., CULTURAL METAPHORS: READINGS, RESEARCH TRANSLATIONS, AND COMMENTARY 9 (Sage Pubs. 2000).

PALMER, JOY A., FIFTY MAJOR THINKERS ON EDUCATION—FROM CONFUCIUS TO DEWEY (Routledge 2001).

PALMER, JOY A., FIFTY MODERN THINKERS ON EDUCATION—FROM PIAGET TO THE PRESENT (Routledge 2003).

PALMER, PARKER, THE COURAGE TO TEACH (1997).

PALMER, PARKER, TO KNOW AS WE ARE KNOWN (HarperOne 1993).

Palomba, Catherine A., *Scholarly Assessment of Student Learning in the Major and General Education*, in BANTA, *supra*.
PAUL, RICHARD W., CRITICAL THINKING—WHAT EVERY PERSON NEEDS TO SURVIVE IN A RAPIDLY CHANGING WORLD 376 (Foundation for Critical Thinking, 3rd ed. 1993).
PAYNE, RUBY K., AND DON L. KRABILL, HIDDEN RULES OF CLASS AT WORK (2002).
PAYNE, RUBY K., UNDERSTANDING LEARNING: THE HOW, THE WHY, THE WHAT (2002).
PAYNE, RUBY K., PHILIP DEVOL, & TERIE DREUSSI SMITH, BRIDGES OUT OF POVERTY: STRATEGIES FOR PROFESSIONALS AND COMMUNITIES (2001).
PAYNE, RUBY K., A FRAMEWORK: UNDERSTANDING AND WORKING WITH STUDENTS AND ADULTS FROM POVERTY (RFT Pub. 1995).
Pedersen, Paul B., *Cross-Cultural Counseling: Developing Culture-Centered Interactions*, in GUILLERMO BERNAL, JOSEPH
Pedersen, Paul B., *Reducing Prejudice and Racism Through Counselor Training as a Primary Prevention Strategy*, in GUILLERMO BERNAL, JOSEPH TRIMBLE, A. KATHLEEN BURLEW, AND FREDERICK LEONG, HANDBOOK OF RACIAL & ETHNIC MINORITY PYSCHOLOGY 621 (Sage Pub. 2003).
Perez, Ruperto M., Mary A. Fukuyama, and Nancy C. Coleman, *Using the Multicultural Guidelines in College Counseling Centers*, in MADONNA G. CONSTANTINE AND DERALD WING SUE, STRATEGIES FOR BUILDING MULTICULTURAL COMPETENCE IN MENTAL HEALTH AND EDUCATIONAL SETTINGS 160 (John Wiley & Sons 2005).
PIAGET, JEAN, PSYCHOLOGY AND EPISTEMOLOGY—TOWARD A THEORY OF KNOWLEDGE (Penguin 1972).
Piomelli, Ascanio, *Cross-Cultural Lawyering by the Book: The Latest Clinical Texts and a Sketch of a Future Agenda*, 4 HASTINGS RACE & POVERTY L.J. 131 (2006).
POLANYI, MICHAEL, PERSONAL KNOWLEDGE (Univ. of Chicago Press 1958).
POLANYI, MICHAEL, THE LOGIC OF LIBERTY (University of Chicago Press 1951).
POLANYI, MICHAEL, THE TACIT DIMENSION (Doubleday & Co. 1967).
Ponterotto, Joseph G., Jaclyn Mendelsohn, and Lonette Belizaire, *Assessing Teacher Multicultural Competence: Self-Report Instruments, Observer Report Evaluations, and a Portfolio Assessment*, in HANDBOOK OF MULTICULTURAL COMPETENCIES IN COUNSELING AND PSYCHOLOGY 191 (Sage Pub. 2003).
PRESSER, STEPHEN B., LAW PROFESSORS: THREE CENTURIES OF SHAPING AMERICAN LAW (West Academic Pub. 2017).
Pressley, Michael, & Karen R. Harris, *Cognitive Strategies Instruction: From Basic Research to Classroom Instruction*, in PATRICIA A. ALEXANDER & PHILIP H. WINNE, HANDBOOK OF EDUCATIONAL PSYCHOLOGY 271 (Lawrence Erlbaum Assocs. Pubs. 2nd ed. 2006).
Quigley, Fran, *Seizing The Disorienting Moment: Adult Learning Theory and the Teaching of Social Justice in Law School Clinics*, 2 CLINICAL L. REV. 37 (1995).
Randall, Vernellia R., *Increasing Retention and Improving Performance: Practical advice on Using Cooperative Learning in Law Schools*, 16 THOMAS M. COOLEY L.REV. 201, 205 (2005).
RANDALL, VERNELLIA R., PLANNING FOR EFFECTIVE LEGAL INSTRUCTION: A WORKBOOK (Carolina Academic Press 2011).
Rice, R. Eugene, and Ann E. Austin, *Organizational Impacts on Faculty Morale and Motivation to Teach*, in PETER SELDIN, HOW ADMINISTRATORS CAN IMPROVE TEACHING 27 (Jossey-Bass 1990).
Ridley, Charles R., Carrie L. Hill, Chalmer E. Thompson, and Alayne J. Ormerod, *Clinical Practice Guidelines in Assessment: Toward an Idiographic Perspective*, in DONALD R. POPE-DAVIS AND HARDIN L.K. COLEMAN, EDS., THE INTERSECTION OF RACE, CLASS, AND GENDER IN MULTICULTURAL COUNSELING 191 (Sage Pubs. 2001).
SAMUEL, GEOFFREY, THE FOUNDATIONS OF LEGAL REASONING 114-115, 117 (Metro 1994).
SARAT, AUSTIN, CATHRINE O. FRANK, & MATTHEW ANDERSON, EDS., TEACHING LAW AND LITERATURE (The Modern Language Assn. of America 2011).
Sarat, Austin, *"... The Law Is All Over": Power, Resistance and the Legal Consciousness of the Welfare Poor*, 2 YALE J.L. & HUMAN. 343 (1990).

SCHEFFLER, ISRAEL, CONDITIONS OF KNOWLEDGE—AN INTRODUCTION TO EPISTEMOLOGY AND EDUCATION (Scott, Foresman and Co. 1965).

Schommer, Marlene, *An Emerging Conceptualization of Epistemological Beliefs and Their Role in Learning*, in KENNETH A. FELDMAN & MICHAEL B. PAULSEN, TEACHING AND LEARNING IN THE COLLEGE CLASSROOM 173 (2d ed. Pearson Custom Pub. 1998).

Schraw, Gregory, *Knowledge: Structures and Processes*, in PATRICIA A. ALEXANDER & PHILIP H. WINNE, HANDBOOK OF EDUCATIONAL PSYCHOLOGY 259 (Lawrence Erlbaum Assocs. Pubs. 2nd ed. 2006).

SCHWARTZ, MICHAEL HUNTER, EXPERT LEARNING FOR LAW STUDENTS (Carolina Academic Press 2d ed. 2008).

SCHWARTZ, MICHAEL HUNTER, SOPHIE M. SPARROW, & GERALD F. HESS, TEACHING LAW BY DESIGN: ENGAGING STUDENTS FROM THE SYLLABUS TO THE FINAL EXAM 2ND ED. (Carolina Academic Press 2017).

SEDBERRY, STEVEN R., LAW SCHOOL LABYRINTH: A GUIDE TO MAKING THE MOST OF YOUR LEGAL EDUCATION 3D. ED. (Sedberry 2015).

Seielstad, Andrea M., *Community Building as a Means of Teaching Creative, Cooperative, and Complex Problem Solving in Clinical Education*, 8 CLINICAL L.REV. 445 (2002).

SELDIN, PETER, THE TEACHING PORTFOLIO: A PRACTICAL GUIDE TO IMPROVED PERFORMANCE AND PROMOTION/TENURE DECISIONS (Anker Pub. 2004).

SHAFIROFF, IRA L., FIRST YEAR LAW SCHOOL SUCCESS: LAW SCHOOL THINKING, ESSAY EXAM WRITING, AND ANALYSIS (BARBRI 2011).

SHERR, AVROM, RICHARD MOORHEAD, & HILARY SOMMERLAD, EDS., LEGAL EDUCATION AT THE CROSSROADS: EDUCATION AND THE LEGAL PROFESSION (Routledge 2017).

Shestack, Jerome J., *President's Message: Pervasive Professionalism Must be Part of Legal Education*, 84 A.B.A. J. 6 (1998).

SHULMAN, LEE, THE WISDOM OF PRACTICE: ESSAYS ON TEACHING, LEARNING, AND LEARNING TO TEACH (Jossey-Bass 2004).

Shulman, Lee S., *Signature Pedagogies in the Professions*, 134(3) DAEDALUS 52, 56 (2005).

SKEMP, RICHARD, INTELLIGENCE, LEARNING, AND ACTION—A FOUNDATION FOR THEORY AND PRACTICE IN EDUCATION (John Wiley & Sons 1979).

SMITH, BARBARA LEIGH, & JOHN MCCANN, EDS., REINVENTING OURSELVES—INTERDISCIPLINARY EDUCATION, COLLABORATIVE LEARNING, AND EXPERIMENTATION IN HIGHER EDUCATION (Anker Publishing 2001).

Smith, Ronald, *Formative Evaluation and the Scholarship of Teaching and Learning*, in NEW DIRECTIONS FOR TEACHING AND LEARNING 51 (John Wiley & Sons, Inc. 2001).

Smith, Sean J., and Eric D. Jones, *The Obligation to Provide Assistive Technology: Enhancing General Curriculum Access*, 28 J.L. & EDUC. 247 (1999).

Sparrow, Sophie M., *Describing the Ball: Improve Teaching by Using Rubrics—Explicit Grading Criteria*, 2004 MICH. ST. L. REV. 1.

STELLJES, ANDREW, SERVICE-LEARNING AND COMMUNITY ENGAGEMENT—COGNITIVE DEVELOPMENTAL LONG-TERM SOCIAL CONCERN (Cambria Press 2008).

STEVENS, ROBERT, LAW SCHOOL: LEGAL EDUCATION IN AMERICAN FROM THE 1850S TO THE 1980S (Univ. North Carolina Press 1983).

STROPUS, RUTA K., & CHARLOTTE D. TAYLOR, BRIDGING THE GAP BETWEEN COLLEGE AND LAW SCHOOL—STRATEGIES FOR SUCCESS 3RD ED. (Carolina Academic Press 2014).

SOCKETT, HUGH, THE MORAL BASE FOR TEACHER PROFESSIONALISM (Teachers College Press 1993).

STEVENS, ROBERT, LAW SCHOOL: LEGAL EDUCATION IN AMERICAN FROM THE 1850S TO THE 1980S (Univ. North Carolina Press 1983).

STUCKEY, ROY, AND OTHERS, BEST PRACTICES FOR LEGAL EDUCATION: A VISION AND A ROAD MAP (Clinical Legal Education Association 2007).

STOLOVITCH, HAROLD D., AND ERICA J. KEEPS, EDS., HANDBOOK OF HUMAN PERFORMANCE TECHNOLOGY (2nd ed. Jossey-Bass Pfeifer 1999).

STRAUSS, PETER L., LEGAL METHODS: UNDERSTANDING AND USING CASES AND STATUTES 3ᴿᴰ ED. (Foundation Press 2014).

SULLIVAN, WILLIAM M., ANNE COLBY, JUDITH WELCH WEGNER, LLOYD BOND, & LEE S. SHULMAN, EDUCATING LAWYERS: PREPARATION FOR THE PROFESSION OF LAW (Jossey-Bass 2007).

SUSSKIND, GERALD, THE END OF LAWYERS? (Oxford Univ. Press 2008).

TALASKI, RICHARD A., ED., CRITICAL REASONING IN CONTEMPORARY CULTURE (SUNY Press 1992).

TAMANAHA, BRIAN Z., FAILING LAW SCHOOLS (University of Chicago Press 2012).

TANAKA, GREG, THE INTER-CULTURAL CAMPUS—TRANSCENDING CULTURE & POWER IN AMERICAN HIGHER EDUCATION (Peter Lang Pub. 2007).

THOMSON, DAVID I.C., LAW SCHOOL 2.0: LEGAL EDUCATION FOR A DIGITAL AGE (LexisNexis 2008).

Todd, Adam G., *Academic Support Programs: Effective Support Through a Systemic Approach*, 38 GONZAGA L.REV. 187 (2003).

Treuthart, Mary Pat, *Resolving a Conundrum: Incorporating Service-Learning into a Women and the Law Course*, in BALLIET, BARBARA J., & KERRISSA HEFFERNAN, THE PRACTICE OF CHANGE—CONCEPTS AND MODELS FOR SERVICE-LEARNING IN WOMEN'S STUDIES 191 (American Association for Higher Education 2000).

TRIMBLE, A. KATHLEEN BURLEW, AND FREDERICK LEONG, HANDBOOK OF RACIAL & ETHNIC MINORITY PYSCHOLOGY (Sage Pub. 2003).

UDELHOFEN, SUSAN, KEYS TO CURRICULUM MAPPING—STRATEGIES AND TOOLS TO MAKE IT WORK (Corwin Press 2005).

URBINA, SEBASTIAN, LEGAL METHOD AND THE RULE OF LAW (Kluwer Law Intl. 2002).

Vasquez, Melba J.T., *Independent Practice Settings and the Multicultural Guidelines*, in MADONNA G. CONSTANTINE AND DERALD WING SUE, STRATEGIES FOR BUILDING MULTICULTURAL COMPETENCE IN MENTAL HEALTH AND EDUCATIONAL SETTINGS 91 (John Wiley & Sons 2005).

WAKE FOREST LAW REVIEW, REVISITING LANGDELL: LEGAL EDUCATION REFORM AND THE LAWYER'S CRAFT (2016).

Wang, Vivian Ota, *Holding up Half the Sky: Reproductive Decision Making by Asian Women in America*, in DONALD R. POPE-DAVIS AND HARDIN L.K. COLEMAN, EDS., THE INTERSECTION OF RACE, CLASS, AND GENDER IN MULTICULTURAL COUNSELING 71 (Sage Pubs. 2001).

WEHLBURG, CATHERINE M., MEAINGFUL COURSE REVISION—ENHANCING ACADEMIC ENGAGEMENT USING STUDENT LEARNING DATA (Anker Pub. Co. 2006).

Weisser, Phil, & Bryce Wilson, *Law School Innovation*, in ROUNDTABLE SERIES ON ENTREPRENEURSHIP, INNOVATION, AND PUBLIC POLICY (May 2016).

Weiss, Stephen E., *Negotiating with "Romans,"* in GANNON, MARTIN J., CULTURAL METAPHORS: READINGS, RESEARCH TRANSLATIONS, AND COMMENTARY 129 (Sage Pubs. 2000).

WEST, ROBIN, TEACHING LAW: JUSTICE, POLITICS, AND THE DEMANDS OF PROFESSIONALISM (Cambridge Univ. Press 2014).

YELON, STEPHEN L., POWERFUL PRINCIPLES OF INSTRUCTION (Longman Pubs. 1996).

ZEIGLER, DONALD H., HOW I TEACH: SUCCESSFUL TECHNIQUES FOR THE LAW SCHOOL CLASSROOM (Tribeca Square Press 2008).

Zinn, Herbert I., *Nets and Parachutes: Lawyer Training and Mentoring*, in JEFFREY R. SIMMONS, LIFE, LAW AND THE PURSUIT OF BALANCE: A LAWYER'S GUIDE TO QUALITY OF LIFE (ABA/ Maricopa County Bar Assn. 1997).

Appendix A

BLOOM'S TAXONOMY OF EDUCATIONAL OBJECTIVES

Level	Competence	Skills Demonstrated	Objectives Cues
1	Knowledge	observation and recall of information; knowledge of dates, events, places; knowledge of major ideas; mastery of subject matter	list, define, tell, describe, identify, show, label, collect, examine, tabulate, quote, name, who, when, where
2	Comprehension	understand information; grasp meaning; translate knowledge into new context; interpret facts; compare, contrast; order, group, infer causes; predict consequences	summarize, describe interpret, contrast, predict, associate, distinguish, estimate, differentiate, discuss, extend.
3	Application	use information; use methods, concepts, theories in new situations; solve problems using	apply demonstrate, calculate, complete, illustrate, show,

		required skills or knowledge	solve, examine, modify, relate, change, classify, experiment, discover
4	Analysis	seeing patterns; organization of parts; recognition of hidden meanings; identification of components	analyze, separate, order, explain, connect, classify, arrange, divide, compare, select, explain, infer
5	Synthesis	use old ideas to create new ones; generalize from given facts; relate knowledge from several areas; predict, draw conclusions	combine, integrate, modify, rearrange, substitute, plan, create, design, invent, what if?, compose, formulate, prepare, generalize, rewrite
6	Evaluation	compare and discriminate between ideas; assess values of theories, presentations; make choices based on reasoned argument; verify value of evidence; recognize subjectivity	assess, decide, rank, grade, test, measure, recommend, convince, select, judge, explain, discriminate, support, conclude, compare, summarize

Appendix B

Syllabus Checklist

Consider this checklist of what you might include in your syllabus. Items do not need to be in any specific order:

____ Course title

____ Course number

____ Number of credits

____ Day, time, and place of class sessions

____ Course instructor

____ Instructor's qualifications

____ Office location

____ Office hours

____ At least one method of contacting instructor

____ Brief description of the course

____ Course prerequisites

____ Statement of how the course aligns with the curriculum

____ Required textbook

____ Recommended materials including the location of each

- ____ Course goals
- ____ Course learning objectives
- ____ Schedule of readings, papers, projects, etc.
- ____ Form of assessments
- ____ Criteria for grading
- ____ Day, time, and location for final exam
- ____ Statement encouraging students to see you outside of class
- ____ Description of and rationale for your teaching methods
- ____ Special procedures or rules for this class
- ____ Advice on how to read class materials
- ____ Advice on how to study for quizzes and exams
- ____ Specific criteria for graded assignments
- ____ Statement on incomplete coursework
- ____ Information on special services

Appendix C

Exam-Format Checklist

1. Instructions concerning student exam ID numbers should be on the COVER SHEET of the exam with a place for students to fill in their exam ID numbers.

TIME

2. Be sure that the COVER SHEET correctly identifies the term. If the exam is for Trinity Term 2008, then indicate "Trinity Term 2008" and not some prior term. Reusing cover sheets from old exams leads to this and other common errors.

3. Be sure that the exam day, date, and time are correct on the COVER SHEET to the exam.

4. Although technically correct, avoid the use of "12:00 P.M." to indicate the noon hour. Thus, a three-credit-class exam that begins at 9 a.m. should indicate "9:00 A.M. TO 12:00 NOON," not "9:00 A.M. TO 12:00 P.M."

5. State the number of minutes for the exam precisely (165 minutes for a three-credit course or 110 minutes for a two-credit course, for example). But state the clock times on the hours, not to the precise minute. Thus, a two-credit-class exam that begins at 6 p.m. should indicate "6:00 P.M. TO 8:00 P.M.," not "6:00 P.M. to 7:50 P.M." Proctors need a few minutes to start and stop the exam.

6. If you state on the COVER SHEET and in the body of the exam recommended times for each question or series of questions, then be sure that:

a. the same time recommendations are used on the COVER SHEET and in the body of the exam, meaning that the recommendations are consistent; and

b. the recommended times total the available time for the full exam. Do not recommend times that exceed the time available to complete the exam.

MATERIALS

7. Be sure that the COVER SHEET clearly states what materials are to be turned in to the proctors at the end of the exam time.

8. Be sure that tables, appendices, statutes, and other materials that are supposed to be a part of the final exam materials are included with the exam and placed in the paginated order where they will be seen and used by students for the appropriate questions. Students overlook until the end of the exam materials placed at the end of the exam.

9. If any materials or equipment are permitted in the exam room such as calculators, code books, notes, etc., then list those items on the COVER SHEET.

PAGINATION

10. Insert PAGE NUMBERS at bottom, middle, but not on the COVER SHEET.

11. The PAGE NUMBERS at the bottom of each page should MATCH the number of pages stated in the INSTRUCTIONS on the COVER SHEET with the cover sheet indicating not to count the first page.

12. Insert PAGE BREAKS at the end of every page. Then the formatting will not move.

13. Be sure that the COVER SHEET correctly lists the number of pages. When the COVER SHEET states, "This exam contains 18 pages," be sure that there are 18 pages.

14. If you have two pages of instructions, please so indicate on your COVER SHEET.

QUESTIONS

15. Be sure that questions are numbered sequentially (1, 2, 3, etc., or A, B, C, D) without skips (1, 2, 4) or repeats (1, 2, 2).

16. Be consistent between the way the questions are identified on the COVER SHEET and in the body of the exam. Watch for COVER SHEETS identifying questions by Roman numerals I, II, III, etc., when the same questions in the body of the exam are numbered 1, 2, 3, etc.

17. If you reuse and tumble your multiple-choice questions, then make sure questions which are in a series stay together or are rejoined after the tumble so that questions do not become separated from facts given in the previous question or questions.

18. Make sure multiple-choice answers are not bolded or noted in any manner in the final exam.

POINTS AND ANSWERS

19. Be sure that the available exam points on the COVER SHEET are consistent with the points reflected in the headings in the body of the exam. If the COVER SHEET states, "Question 1...........20 points," then the heading for Question 1 in the body of the exam should also state "20 points" and not some other number of points.

20. Be sure that the points add up correctly on the COVER SHEET and in the body of the exam.

21. Put ellipses ("...................") on the COVER SHEET between the question number and the available points. Thus: "Question 1........................20 points."

22. Clearly indicate where students are to place their answers—for instance, multiple-choice answers on the Scantron sheet or in the blue book/typed exam, short answers in the blue book/typed exam or on the exam itself, and essays in the blue book/typed exam.

Please proofread the final copy of your exam and have others proofread your exam. Please contact the exam administrator if you have questions.

Appendix D

Grading Checklist

____ **I prepared a detailed answer key to accompany each bluebook.**

    ____ The answer key matched the final exam in categories and points.

____ **I recorded all grades on my worksheets and spreadsheets.**

    ____ I investigated any missing bluebooks or Scantron results

____ **My scoring of answers matched the detailed answer key by categories and points.**

    ____ I evaluated and assigned points for all categories shown on the answer key.

    ____ The points awarded reflect the points available (no total available points error).

____ **I accurately calculated final scores from my individual scoring of answers.**

    ____ I included all scores (multiple-choice, short answer, and essay) in the final score.

    ____ I confirmed the accuracy of the mathematic tabulations.

    ____ I properly added score to score.

    ____ I properly weighted scores (like number of points per multiple choice).

___ **I properly sorted scores when ranking highest to lowest.**

___ **I properly assigned the grade ranges.**

    ___ Grade ranges match the grading definitions in the student policy manual.

    ___ There is a grade range for every available grade (A, A-, B, B-, C, C-, D, and F).

    ___ The grade ranges are continuous, without gaps between ranges.

    ___ I can justify any departure from uniform grade ranges (A- to C).

    ___ My overall GPA is consistent with historical norms or can be justified.

    ___ My overall GPA is consistent with department norms or can be justified.

___ **I properly transposed ranges and scores from worksheet to grade sheet.**

    ___ Each exam number on the grade sheet matches my worksheet.

___ **There is a score for every exam number on the grade sheet except for missed exams.**

___ **I filled in the ranges at the bottom of the grade sheet (matches my worksheet).**

___ **I indicated on the grade sheet the exam number that won the certificate of merit.**

___ **My grade sheet was reviewed by the associate or assistant dean.**

___ **Any required departmental review or approval has been obtained.**

___ **I signed the grade sheet.**

___ **I completed grading before grades were due, allowing time for review and processing.**

Appendix E

A Common Language of Learning

A professional learning community (students, faculty, staff, and administrators) shares understanding and purpose by sharing language. Consider the following language of legal instruction, including both terms of pedagogy and learning culture. Decide what words you would use when you teach, speak, write, and collaborate. Use and discuss them with your colleagues. Develop a common language of instruction.

Acculturation	Comprehensive	Domain
Affective	Conclusion	Encoding
Analogy	Criterion	Encouragement
Analysis	Cross-cultural	Enculturation
Application	Cross-discipline	Enjoyment
Assessment	Cultural	Epistemology
Bias	Curiosity	Ethic
Challenge	Depth	Evaluation
Class	Dicta	Exploration
Cognitive	Differentiate	Foster
Collaboration	Dimension	Framework
Collaborative	Discern	Goals
learning	Discriminate	Hierarchical
Competency	Diverse	Historical

Holding	Persistence	Self-reflection
Humility	Policies	Sensible
Inferential	Practice Preparation	Sensitivity
Instructional	Prejudice	Service
Integration	Principles	Shared mission
Integrity	Procedural	Shared vision
Intellectual	Professional	Skill
Intentionality	Professional development	Socioeconomic
Interaction	Professional identity	Stereotype
Issues	Promote	Study
Issue Spotting	Purpose Pedagogy	Subjective
Judgment	Reasoning	Substantiate
Knowledge	Recall	Substantive
Learning	Recognize	Support
Literal	References	Synthesis
Mastery	Reflect	Team learning
Methodology	Register	Terminology
Misattribution	Relationship	Theory
Mission	Relevant	Traditional
Monocultural	Reliability	Trust
Multicultural	Resource	Truth-seeking
Mnemonic	Responsible	Understanding
Norm	Rigorous	Unity
Objective	Rules	Validity
Ontology	Schema	Virtue
Partnering		Vision

Appendix F

Glossary

Abductive: Having to do with a process of reasoning that uses known data to generate hypotheses guiding further investigation. "Abductive reasoning helps lawyers decide what evidence to pursue." Contrast with "inductive" and "deductive."

Acculturation: adaptations in practices, values, and beliefs one experiences when influenced by substantial contact with a culture unlike one's own.

Affective: Having to do with the student's displayed manner. The way in which a student exhibits learning. "Your class recitation shows strong affective skills." Contrast with cognitive.

Analogic: Reasoning by pattern, image, or picture imposed over given facts. "Expert professional judgment is often performed analogically." Contrast with analytic.

Analytic: A systematic manner of reasoning by breaking claims down into definitions, factors, and elements. "Legal reasoning is typically expressed analytically." Contrast with analogic.

Application: A middle-order cognitive skill above knowledge (encoding) and understanding (rephrasing) but below synthesis and evaluation. "Your mid-term results suggest that you may need to work more on application."

Assessment: The practice of studying results to improve instruction. A feedback loop. "Cooley Law School's vision includes the assessment of instruction."

Bias: making assumptions (positive or negative) about a person based on class, culture, or other presumed group characteristics. Compare to "prejudice."

Challenge: To adjust instruction to the student's outer margin of learning in order to maximize the opportunity for growth.

Class: a grouping of clients traditionally by income level such as lower-income, middle-income, upper-income, etc., in order to infer statuses helpful to informed legal advice.

Cognitive: Having to do with the student's internal thinking and reasoning. The way in which a student processes concepts internally. "Let's talk about the cognitive skills you will need to practice in this area." Contrast with affective.

Collaboration: Interactive learning among peers to reduce the isolated narrowness and subjectivity inherent in a single view.

Competency: An ability level sufficient to accomplish the designated skill in a practice setting. "Our practice-preparation mission places competency at the core of instruction."

Comprehensive: Covering the breadth of a subject.

Conclusion: A statement reflecting the result of the application of a legal rule. "Analysis typically requires a conclusion as to which party will prevail when the rule is applied to a dispute."

Criterion: The standard against which a student's performance is measured. "A common criterion in code-based courses is that the statement of the rule be consistent with the applicable portion of the code."

Cross-cultural: relating to interaction between two different sets of common practices, values, and beliefs of groups identifiable by race, class, locale, and other characteristic or attribute.

Cross-discipline: Making use of a concept or construct from outside the particular legal field. "Cross-discipline studies can add context and dimension to legal education."

Cultural: based on or influenced by the common practices, values, and beliefs of a group that is identifiable by race, class, locale, and other characteristic or attribute.

Curiosity: The innate and heartfelt desire to encounter new subjects and to learn.

Depth: Beyond the surface into the richness and profundity of a subject.

Dicta: A statement of law in a court opinion that is not necessary to the case's outcome and may therefore be suspect as authority. "The court's discussion of venue is dicta, so we might question its reliability."

Differentiate: To adjust instructional activities to meet the learning styles and needs of particular students. "To differentiate instruction on difficult subjects tends to help more students comprehend the matter at hand."

Dimension: The conceptual field of knowledge, skills, or ethics within which an instructional activity fits. "Exposure to a full range of professional identities falls within the ethics dimension of our program."

Discern: To recognize, conceptualize, or envision effectively in the exercise of professional skill and judgment. "Our instruction has as a broad goal to help students discern effectively and wisely in practice."

Discriminate: To sort on the basis of the ability or inability to exercise a specific skill. "Our test items are designed to discriminate at just the level of skill that will predict bar passage."

Diverse: client characteristics, attributes, and practices that vary in a significant way likely to affect legal advice, from those which a lawyer usually experiences.

Domain: The conceptual field within which a particular skill may lie. "The mixed knowledge/ethics domain skill you are attempting here may be a challenge."

Encoding: The cognitive process by which newly acquired information is stored. "Changes in viewpoint can aid effective encoding by increasing the number of retrieval routes."

Encouragement: Active support of and inspiration for learning.

Enculturation: the unnoticed immersion of a person into habits and practices that influence the person's conduct toward others.

Enjoyment: A state of satisfaction associated with the acquisition of knowledge and skill.

Epistemology: The study of knowledge. "The dominant epistemology of law practice centers on analytical skill."

Ethic: The basis, system, or rationale on which a lawyer or client makes evaluative judgments. "Instrumentalism, although dominant, is only one professional ethic among a number of others."

Evaluation: A higher-level cognitive skill (above knowledge, understanding, and application) having to do with making judgments about the wisdom or efficacy of a result under a certain formulation of a rule.

Exploration: To seek familiarity with a subject by active interaction with it in a variety of manners. "We encourage exploration of this subject primarily through hypothesis evaluation and role play."

Foster: To protect, promote, and support in learning.

Framework: an organized and well-thought-out conceptual structure a lawyer can use to inform and guide the lawyer's professional attitude and practices toward a client.

Goals: The overarching results sought by a program of instruction. "Our goals here include that you would develop a self-reflective capacity and acquire a meta-cognitive attitude toward learning."

Hierarchical: Arranged in order of level or priority. "Thinking of these categories as hierarchical can aid encoding."

Historical: Having reference to a meaningful past capable of informing the present and future.

Holding: A statement of law in a court opinion material to the case's outcome and therefore reliable as authority. "The holding of this opinion is that intent transfers among traditional intentional torts."

Humility: An attribute preserving the ability of a person to learn from others.

Inferential: Drawing reasonable or presumed meanings from contexts in which they are not directly stated. The mid-level of reading above literal and below evaluative. "This somewhat vague case definitely requires an inferential reading."

Instructional: Conducted for the purpose of aiding learning. "Our primary instructional activity today will be group discussion of problems."

Integration: The bringing together in meaningful relationship of different dimensions of a program of instruction. "We seek the integration of knowledge with skills and ethics."

Integrity: A quality of consistency between the thoughts, words, and actions of a person.

Intellectual: Having to do with an active and positive life of the mind.

Intentionality: The carrying out and forward of a purposeful and wise plan for learning.

Interaction: Positive and supportive communication supporting learning.

Issues: Reasonable points of contention in a legal dispute. "Although they are pretty confidently resolved, I would say that the issues in this case include jurisdiction and venue."

Issue Spotting: The skill of identifying reasonable points of contention out of a client's recitation or fact set. "Given the variety of ways in which these problems arise, issue spotting is a skill critical to this class."

Judgment: The professional skill of applying a body of knowledge to an unresolved dispute arising out of a client's recitation or fact set. "The exercise of professional judgment includes identifying important ethical concerns."

Knowledge: The legal information out of which understanding develops and applications can be made. "Our knowledge base includes not only the code provisions but interpreting regulations."

Learning: An unavoidable and necessary, creative, and life- and meaning-giving activity. "Because we are a school of access and diversity, we are deliberate in serving a variety of learning styles."

Literal: Drawing only those meanings that are expressed in the speech or text. The lowest level of reading below inferential and evaluative. "You will do better to keep your reading of this statute to the literal."

Mastery: That level of competence that would give ready confidence to a client when the skill is exercised in the field. "This capstone course seeks your mastery of this narrow field."

Methodology: The study of the process or means by which a task is accomplished. "Methodology is important in this area, and so we will consider several alternative means."

Misattribution: assigning the wrong goals, objectives, or intent to a client because of bias, prejudice, or misunderstanding.

Mission: An institutionally defined purpose relating to the education of students.

Mnemonic: A memorable word or series of letters constructed for the purpose of assisting one's ability to recall a list of terms. "Try building a mnemonic out of these factors if you think that you will be unable to generate them on your own."

Monocultural: representative of the common practices, values, and beliefs of a single group identifiable by race, class, locale, and other characteristic or attribute.

Multicultural: representative of the common practices, values, and beliefs of a variety of groups identifiable by race, class, locale, and other characteristic or attribute.

Norm: A group-averaged standard or capability against which performance is measured. "There is an unresolved question whether exams should be criterion-referenced or norm-referenced."

Objective: A statement describing the expected practice-based performance, the conditions under which it is to occur, and the criteria by which it is judged. "Our objective for this week's instruction is shown on the board."

Ontology: Study of the origin, foundations, or beginning of the matter under consideration. "An ontology can be helpful to a synthetic level of understanding within a field."

Partnering: The coming together of diverse individuals or organizations for the purpose of promoting related goals and interests.

Pedagogy: The study of teaching and learning. "We share a commitment to learned pedagogy."

Persistence: The quality of continuing forward toward mastery of a learning goal or challenge when its attainment appears doubtful.

Policies: The social interests to be served by a certain law or rule. That which justifies a law. "What policies would you identify as supporting this rule?"

Practice Preparation: Coordinated acts of learning having the goal of enabling one to perform competent legal service in pursuit of laudable goals.

Prejudice: holding negative feelings about a person based on class, culture, locale, and other presumed group characteristics, and expressing those negative feelings in treatment of the person.

Principles: Shared underlying beliefs about justice that are used to justify more specific rule and law formulations. "Principles of fairness and reciprocity support the rule and outcome in this case."

Procedural: Having to do with the means or process used to decide a dispute or accomplish a task. "The shortened response time raises several procedural concerns including whether the defendant can retain counsel in time to answer."

Professional: based on or influenced by the approved practices of skilled and ethical lawyers.

Professional development: Continual and intentional activities and practices undertaken for the self-reflective purpose of improving skills. "Cooley Law School supports the professional development of its faculty."

Professional identity: The accumulation of observable attributes and characteristics that mark one's moral, ethical, and general reputation in the community. "Today's instruction will help you explore aspects of professional identity."

Promote: To act with the purpose of bringing another closer to their stated goal.

Purpose: The point or end toward which, or the foundational understanding around which, one directs volition or intent.

Reasoning: The methods or means by which a conclusion is supported through the application of law to facts. "Although the case's conclusion is justifiable, the reasoning is under-developed leaving us uncertain of its reliability."

Recall: The ability to bring up in the mind for conscious deliberation laws and other data that have been stored through instruction. "Recall is aided by encoding several routes of accessibility."

Recognize: To bring into one's mind or mental vision with clarity enabling further conceptualization.

References: the traditions, concepts, and meanings a person's communication, demeanor, dress, and other observable characteristics would suggest to a skilled and sensitive observer.

Reflect: To mull or ponder in an active manner that seeks to bring about a resolution or reveal possible ends.

Register: language levels or patterns reflecting a person's habits of thinking. There are at least five recognized language registers.

Relationship: the inherent nature and essential quality of the ongoing interaction between two or more persons.

Relevant: Having the capability of influencing or changing the outcome of the issue under consideration.

Reliability: An appropriate connection between the subject of the test item and the course's instructional objective. "The reliability of this multiple-choice question is doubtful, because its subject is not one of our priority points of instruction."

Responsible: Being accountable by act, agreement, or relationship for the outcome of a learning event.

Resources: the broad variety of available means (finances, contacts, skills, etc.) by which students further their own objectives.

Rigorous: The quality of being tested and assured to a high degree.

Rules: Specific, subordinate, authoritative statements generally applicable within a field of law. "The rules you must know in practice include all of those having to do with when a confidential matter may and must be disclosed."

Schema: A conceptual structure or scaffold by which a law student or lawyer approaches an issue. "Developing a prioritized list of factors is one schema through which you can organize, recall, and apply this learning."

Self-reflection: A sober-minded and wise assessing of one's own quality, nature, and merit or lack thereof.

Sensible: In accord with the experience and wisdom of numbers and ages.

Sensitivity: The quality of being observant, aware, and capable of making positive use of subtle differentiations.

Service: The act of setting one's own interests aside in order to promote the interests of another.

Shared mission: Agreement on an institutionally defined goal.

Shared vision: Common insight on the general subordinate principles that will achieve an institutional goal.

Skill: A discrete and specific ability or performance requiring the application of legal knowledge in a new circumstance. "The skill this instruction supports is the ability to quickly organize and display the analysis of an intentional tort claim."

Socioeconomic: related to the person's social environment and economic status such as majority homeless, minority low-income, immigrant middle-income, etc.

Stereotype: an incorrect image of a person constructed from prior experience with other clients assumed to be alike, and likely to adversely affect the relationship.

Study: The act of creatively devoting one's efforts toward learning a specific subject or skill.

Support: The act of giving help or assistance to another's learning.

Subjective: Having to do with the knowledge and viewpoint of the person whose conduct is under consideration. "If we applied a subjective test, the defendant would clearly have been justified in taking that action."

Substantiate: To supply the necessary evidence or justification to make apparent and acceptable the asserted conclusion. "Substantiate your conclusions by addressing each element in its turn."

Substantive: Having to do with the doctrinal law, rules, or grounds on which, or ends toward which, a decision is made. "Now that the procedural issue is resolved, we must turn to the issue's substantive consideration."

Synthesis: The act of drawing together laws, rules, and doctrines within a larger field that may at first appear disparate. A higher-order skill above knowledge, understanding, application, and analysis. "You might base this subject's synthesis on a historical or moral view."

Team learning: Acquiring new skills through instructional activities where the teaching or guiding expertise is shared among members of the group. "The law firm format of this class provides opportunities for team learning."

Terminology: The words and phrases a learning community shares to accomplish the instructional tasks. "Consider carefully the terminology in this unit to be able to distinguish its proper use."

Theory: A testable premise or assertion supported by reasoning or grounds. "Please explain to us the theory that justified the defendant's appeal."

Traditional: The quality of having been recognized and accepted over a period of time usually extending to generations.

Trust: The quality of a relationship in which there is mutual commitment and devotion to one another's well-being.

Truth-seeking: Efforts in pursuit of transferable, useful, and unimpeachable understanding.

Understanding: The capability to rephrase and express acquired knowledge. "You need not recall these definitions verbatim but must demonstrate your understanding by putting them in your own words."

Unity: The coming together of diverse minds around a common understanding and goal.

Validity: A test item's capability of accurately measuring the performance the item is designed to test. "The answer choices for this multiple-choice question seem too much alike to assure the question's validity."

Virtue: Goodness inhering in an individual by practiced acts of beneficence.

Vision: The comprehension and statement of a principle that if carried into effect will further a fundamental goal.